PEACE be unto thy SOUL

PEACE *be* *unto* *thy* SOUL

A Practical Guide to Overcoming Grief, Loss, and Disappointment

JOSEPH L. BISHOP PhD

Covenant Communications, Inc.

I gratefully dedicate this book to my sons: Greg, Bob, Mike,
Steve, and Scott, whose uncompromising love and support continually
assisted me through my "darkening trials," and to those many others who, in
their monumental struggle to overcome their personal
grief, took the time to teach me how to do the same.

Cover image: *The Last Rays of Sunshine* © Anita Stizzoli. Courtesy istockphoto.com.

Cover design copyright © 2012 by Covenant Communications, Inc.

Published by Covenant Communications, Inc.
American Fork, Utah

Printed in the United States of America
First Printing: September 2012

18 17 16 15 14 13 12   10 9 8 7 6 5 4 3 2 1

ISBN 978-1-60861-480-6

Table of Contents

FOREWORD

I HAVE WORKED IN THE trauma field as a therapist for more than twenty-five years. Over that period, I have witnessed individuals deal with pain and loss that seemed too much for humans to bear. With time and experience, I have gradually come to realize that the human spirit is stronger than anything that can happen to it . . . *if correct principles and God are permitted to strengthen it*. Gratefully, that is the thrust of *Peace Be unto Thy Soul*.

This book is a refreshing and important contribution to those who are suffering—and it comes at an important time. Therapists are now rethinking how an individual might best move from paralysis and despair to making a new life and what processes should be involved. These painful and growth-enhancing procedures of searching, developing new perspectives, and allowing each grief survivor to find his or her own way out of that devastating grief dovetail nicely with the principles explained and illustrated in this book.

The uniqueness of *Peace Be unto Thy Soul* brings together elements of grieving not generally considered. When one thinks of dealing with terrible losses, it is not customary to address judging, fear, self-deception, living in the present, expectations, the natural man, or gratitude, to name a few, as part of the solution. But after reading the book, the impact of these items in one's life is made clear.

The book also makes us aware of the central roles the Atonement of Jesus Christ and the Spirit play in our healing. Spiritual truths can infuse life's problems with meaning as well as solutions. How many times have we heard someone who has endured loss or adversity say, "I don't know how someone could do it without the gospel." *Peace Be unto Thy Soul* makes much more available those elements of the gospel so needed in dealing with loss.

Using spiritual solutions to remedy everyday problems is not a new concept, but pairing the specific problems of self-imposed grief to specific solutions that are based on gospel principles is a new approach people need to know about. As I read through these pages, I felt grateful as a reader that these gospel resources are being made so widely available in a meaningful and relevant context because they are extremely valuable in our world of loss and grief.

On a more personal note, may I add that I individually benefitted from reading *Peace Be unto Thy Soul.* I resonated with its principles and felt its inspiration. I knew it was a book I would mark, reread, and come back to, one I would reflect on for deeper understanding and application. It is a book I will read with others in mind, gleaning principles I can teach others in my practice as well as in my personal relationships as they are dealing with their grief and losses. This book feels like a gift for me personally at this time in my life. It taps into universal principles that have special relevance to our human condition.

I was with Joseph during some of the challenging times in his wife's fight against cancer and eventual death. I believe a great deal of the synergy between us that generated some of the ideas he drew upon had to do with who he was. His humble and open approach to life, his honesty, humor, and kindness made it possible for us to learn together what principles truly mattered and which were most helpful during such a time when his soul was being tested. From my small investment of lunch once a week with a close friend and colleague, I have received in return this wonderful and timely book. I trust it will find its way into the hands of many who may be searching for their own way to the other side of grief and peace to their souls.

I believe this book by Joseph makes a unique contribution to grief literature. Its approach allows the reader to flexibly apply clear and understandable principles according to his or her own unique responses to grief. All readers can anticipate that applying these timeless principles in this way will lead to an unfolding restoration of their happiness and that it will deepen, enrich, and expand their life. I will absolutely have it in my office and waiting room for me and all others to examine whenever we want.

LARRY D. BEALL, PHD
*Director of the Trauma and
Awareness Treatment Center
Salt Lake City*

PREFACE

OVERCOMING YOUR GRIEF

MANY YEARS AGO I WAS asked to serve on the General Board of the Sunday School. Also serving on that board was another Joseph—Joseph B. Wirthlin. Though he did not often give counsel, when he did, we all listened carefully because he had an ability to see the full scope of the topics we discussed and to anticipate problems as well as point out potential solutions the rest of us would not have seen. His tireless work was evidenced by his well-worn briefcase that seemed to be forever with him—always chock-full of work that had to be done *now*. He was an inspiration to us all.

I mention this other Joseph because it was he who not only helped me properly organize a special event for the Sunday School but who also later helped me with a more personal and serious problem—the subject of which is chronicled in this book. His counsel for this personal matter came in a speech he gave as an apostle at general conference when I was struggling to get over the untimely death of my wife. That sad event had triggered a dark cloud that seemed to follow me wherever I went.

Despite my testimony that life does not end after this mortal existence, try as I might, I could not dislodge my feelings of gloom. I tried to take consolation in knowing that grieving over lost loved ones is natural. In fact, the Lord actually instructs us to "mourn with those that mourn" (Mosiah 18:9). Even our Savior Himself mourned bitterly when He arrived at the tomb of His beloved friend Lazarus. The shortest yet perhaps most poignant verse in the New Testament describes Christ's grief-stricken feelings in two words: "Jesus wept" (John 11:35). And He did not weep sparingly or mildly, for all those who witnessed it said, "Behold how he loved him!" (John 11:36).

Grief is an unavoidable aspect of this mortal existence because, in spite of our testimonies of the plan of salvation, we genuinely miss our loved ones who go on before us. But prolonging such grief or allowing it to become the guiding force in our lives, as did I, is not in accord with the scriptures or good sense. Clearly, the more we understand how grief can become toxic and destructive, the more we will be able to overcome it. That became my quest: to identify the cause of my grief and do something about it.

As luck would have it, I was in a unique place to seriously consider this problem because 1) I was deeply immersed in my own grief, so I knew firsthand what it was like, and 2) I had the advantage of being associated with a group of people whose grief exceeded my own—but who had been successful in overcoming their sorrow. Since they knew the way out and I did not, I correctly reasoned that I could learn from them.

I first become acquainted with these people when they were patients at the Trauma Awareness and Treatment Center (a nonprofit clinic in Salt Lake City) and I was serving on that organization's governing board. Being an educator (and an occasional researcher)—not a psychologist—I could only watch from afar as these patients, under the wise therapy of Dr. Larry D. Beall, the director of the center, fought their way through Kubler-Ross's five stages of grief, which follow:

1. *Denial* (This isn't happening to me!)
2. *Anger* (Why is this happening to me?)
3. *Bargaining* (I promise I'll be a better person *if. . .*)
4. *Depression* (I don't care anymore.)
5. *Acceptance* (I'm ready for whatever comes.)

I soon noticed that some patients seemed to progress through the first four stages with little effort, easily arriving at the final stage of acceptance. That intrigued me. What was it that these people understood that others, including me, did not or *could not?* After reviewing other cases of those who struggled with grief, I found that without exception, those who quickly adjusted to their challenges did so because they saw the first four stages of grief differently from those who seemed to be locked in their grief. Consider this group's typical responses to questions concerning each of the before-mentioned stages of grief:

1. *Denial* (This isn't happening to me!) Response: *Of course it's happening to me!*

2. *Anger* (Why is this happening to me?) Response: *What difference does that make?*

3. *Bargaining* (I promise I'll be a better person *if*. . .) Response: *Ha! Good luck with that.*

4. *Depression* (I don't care anymore.) Response: *Come on. That's not a solution—that's a cop-out.*

5. *Acceptance* (I'm ready for whatever comes.) Response: *Accepting what "is" is the only logical thing to do. Anything less is just self-deception.*

Even more significant was that many of the people whose grief I researched seemed to understand almost intuitively what was causing their grief, thereby making it possible for them to bypass much of their suffering. Take the case of Martha (not her real name), who initially struggled with her grief and then had a breakthrough. She explained:

> It's like a dream I had . . . or maybe it was a revelation. In my dream I was shipwrecked on an island with no one to help me. I was delighted to find a freshwater stream cascading down the lush mountain slope. I also discovered that I could easily catch plenty of fish from the lagoon and that the island was replete with all kinds of tropical fruits and vegetables. The bad news was that some of the fish I caught were actually poisonous, as were some of the fruits and vegetables I picked. As a result of not knowing which foods were bad for me, I often ate the wrong things and made myself sick.
>
> Recognizing that my illness must be caused by something I was eating, I quickly reduced my "diet" to one single item. When that did not make me sick, I added another to my diet to see how that would affect me. In this process, I methodically found those foods that made me ill and then completely eliminated them from my diet. Having learned what was good for me and what was not, life became enjoyable.
>
> When I woke up, I immediately realized I could get rid of my grief the same way I had overcome my illness on that deserted island. I just needed to find out what I was "consuming" (doing) that caused me so much grief and eliminate that from my life. I did that, and life has been sweet ever since.

Another person said it was like a coin with the word *grief* engraved on one side and *happiness* on the other. He explained, "To get rid of your grief, all you have to do is turn the coin over—stop doing the things that create your grief. It's as simple as that."

These insightful people, and many others who seemed to miraculously appear as I traveled through my own journey of discovery, unanimously agreed that many unknowingly create much, if not all, of their own grief. That being true, logic would tell us that those who create their grief can also *stop* creating their grief—it is not something that must be continually endured. But only when they recognize *how* they are making themselves miserable can they discontinue those harmful practices. As I later learned, much of this requires a spiritual understanding as well as personal dedication to become strong, so as to overcome affliction. It is as God has said: "And if men come unto me I will show unto them their weakness. I give unto men weakness that they may be humble . . . for if they humble themselves before me, and have faith in me, then will I make weak things become strong unto them" (Ether 12:27).

Armed with the positive results of my initial research and my desire to recapture some joy in my own life, I continued to search for more of the pieces that would either verify or nullify the initial conclusions of the people who were coping well with their grief. As more data rolled in from this research, it soon became clear that the majority of those who consistently continued to struggle caused unnecessary grief for themselves and for others by their bad choices. And the surprising part was that *none of these people was even slightly aware that they were causing their own misery.*

As the data continued to come forth, I was able to gather an adequate information base and to analyze and organize that data into to a series of governing principles that identified some of the more common errors people choose to make, thus causing themselves grief. Once that was completed, I organized those characteristics into a logical sequence related to the process of their grieving.

For that organizational structure, I again chose to use Kubler-Ross's five stages of grief (I could have used others, for there are several out there). Their program worked well for me because, as I identified the different characteristics that precluded these people from progressing through their grief, I could easily slot them into the appropriate level of Kubler-Ross's five stages of grief. In this way, I could specifically identify what was causing a particular person's grief as well as the level where he had been forced to stop progressing. Of course, for the purposes of this book, I was more interested in finding out how some were able to progress through these stages and quickly arrive at stage five, *acceptance.*

While this book does not address the complexities of clinical depression, nor is it meant to do so, it clearly points the way for readers to find lasting relief from feeling despondent, sad, blue, unhappy, miserable, or down in the dumps—particularly when that grief is unknowingly self-imposed. Finding relief first requires awareness of those things that provoke the grief and then the prescription that will help heal pain and suffering.

But before I get into a more detailed explanation, allow me to give a word of caution. If you choose to consider what is suggested herein (many have done so with confirmed success), please understand that this is not a replacement for your doctor's advice. And if in this process your medical status improves, as did mine, don't make any changes in your medications, regardless of any health improvement, without first consulting your physician. To do so could be dangerous to your health.

INCREASING YOUR HAPPINESS

If you find the cause of your grief and by so doing are able to overcome your afflictions, logically, you will find yourself on the other side of your grief, in a state of happiness. That logical division—1) finding the cause of your grief and what is necessary to overcome it, and 2) finding and increasing your happiness by increasing your level of spirituality—provides the framework for the two major divisions of this book. In the first section, the shift from grief to happiness seems to take place naturally as patients achieve Kubler-Ross's final level of acceptance. The second section emerges when self-inflicted grief is subdued and a new happiness enters your life. At that juncture you will find, as others have expressed it, a higher level of understanding and peace drifting into your life. Because people experience grief and then eventually emerge from it, both opposing worlds are represented in this book.

Another interesting fact emerged in my studies. As I identified the characteristics that contributed to grief, I was, without fail, able to find these same characteristics discussed in the scriptures (as well as in the warning counsel given by the Lord's anointed). Thus, the content of this book is expressed as both a clinical and spiritual treatise. The clinical makes clear the problem; the spiritual makes clear the solution. Out of this mix evolved practical, common-sense guidelines that have proven effective in overcoming feelings of grief and despondency as confirmed by the experiences of those who've grieved and by the scriptures and inspired words of Church leaders. Having my personal studies confirmed by scripture and by God's chosen servants gives me confidence to pass this information on to you—in the hope that you too might find relief.

So if you are grieving the loss of someone, experiencing sadness, or even having bouts of outright depression, unsure if you will ever again feel peace and happiness in your life—or if you simply want to increase your level of happiness—please read this book. Like many others who have applied these principles to their lives, including myself, you may be surprised how quickly you will experience a change for the better.

I will begin my explanation with the story of how I first identified the source of my own seemingly insurmountable grief when my wife died. After all, it was her passing that allowed me to personally test what had been revealed so clearly in my research and in the scriptures and was also the reason she was able to leave me and other family members and loved ones with no observable sorrow, while we, at the same time, were besieged with grief.

ACKNOWLEDGMENTS

Writing a book can be a tedious and lonely task, ranking for me at the same level as having a root canal. Fortunately, I had a support team of very bright and talented people who helped me persevere.

I give heartfelt thanks to Dr. Larry D. Beall, the director of the Trauma Awareness and Treatment Center in Salt Lake City, who first suggested that I chronicle and analyze the "why" of the subject of this book. For more than a year, we met weekly to review these and other concepts. I am also indebted to Dan Hogan and Hyrum Smith, who pointed the way when I was lost in the "dark and dreary world." To Evelyn Jankovich, Rebecca Miller, Kip Davis, and Robert and Helen Wells, for their insightful evaluations of "chapter and verse," I am most appreciative. I am also grateful to my insightful and skillful friends at Covenant Communications—Phil Reschke, whom I have admired for more than thirty years, and my talented editor, Samantha Van Walraven. Finally, I thank my wife, Rena, for her patience and understanding during the long months that I was barricaded in my office. To all of these and many more who appeared in my studies but must go unnamed, I express my sincere appreciation.

Section One

HOW TO OVERCOME YOUR GRIEF

Chapter One

CAROLYN'S PASSING

ON ANY OTHER DAY, IN any other set of circumstances, the morning would have been beautiful. In our new hardtop convertible, my wife, Carolyn, and I were slowly winding our way down the street, away from our well-loved home of twenty-four years. At the corner, some kid yelled, "Nice car, dude!" and gave me a thumbs-up. Normally, I would have honked a brief reply—but not today. Not even the new-car smell of fine leather could cheer me up.

Carolyn was dressed in a brightly colored muumuu that belied our feelings of gloom. A dark cloud hung over us. She rode in silence and moved only once in an attempt to extricate her oxygen line that had somehow become wedged between the seats. I reached over and gave it a tug. The tank in the backseat seemed to yank back, almost as if to say, "Watch it, bud." As I finally managed to free the line, Carolyn smiled a brief thank-you and was lost again in her own thoughts.

Carolyn's health problems started so innocently. At one of her routine gynecological visits, the doctor found some lesions that concerned him. After due consideration, she decided to have them removed. That minor operation went well, and within two weeks she was like her old self. But the doctor was still concerned. "At your age, Carolyn, and with those lesions, we might as well make certain we are ahead of the curve for anything else that might be going on," he said. "I would like you to consider having a total hysterectomy. Take your time deciding. There is no hurry." He was right. There was no hurry. Even though she decided to have the operation, it was already too late.

During the operation—which the surgeon said would be just a routine procedure—the doctor found tumors on the colon, as well as others attached to the fatty tissue of the stomach. The insidious killer was well advanced; it had been quietly sneaking around, growing here and there without notice. Uninvited and unwelcome, it had moved in to stay.

Carolyn immediately started the first round of chemotherapy. We lived in our hope that we were indeed "ahead of the curve"—that we were going to beat this assault or, as the old saying goes, "die trying." How horribly prophetic! The weeks passed. Carolyn continued to lose her hair while the tumor markers rose. We were not ahead of the curve. In fact, we were far behind it.

The second round of chemotherapy resulted in the same lack of success. In the middle of this futile series of treatments, the doctor decided to try a different drug—a much more powerful one. Late one evening, midway through her new treatment, Carolyn's fever spiked to 104.3 degrees. "That's the wonderful thing about chemotherapy," I hopelessly said to myself. "If the cancer doesn't kill you, the treatment will. It's a no-win situation." Somehow, voicing my anger, even to myself, seemed to help. But the hopelessness soon returned.

Since Carolyn's doctor was on vacation, we immediately called the doctor's on-call replacement. He sleepily mumbled something about the treatment causing her high temperature and said he would clear his appointments so that he could see her early in the morning. Knowing that a doctor does not drop his appointments unless a situation is serious, we took this as a clear sign that she was in trouble.

The next morning we drove in silence to the doctor's office to keep our appointment. The wind was softly blowing through Carolyn's short hair— the result of her chemotherapy. She finally broke her silence. "It's so hard to stop planning," she said. "We have our anniversary, my birthday, and your birthday all coming up in the next few weeks."

"We'll make all of these events and many more," I said hopefully. But my words rang false and were all but swept away with the wind. She knew it . . . and so did I.

When we arrived at the doctor's office, the doctor and several members of the hospice staff were waiting for us. They immediately took us into a room, closed the sliding glass door that separated us from the long rows of recliners where patients were receiving their chemotherapy, and pulled the curtains. Without preamble, the on-call doctor put Carolyn's lab reports aside, took her by the hand, and softly announced, "Carolyn, you are dying." While we were fearful of Carolyn's condition, the abruptness of the death sentence uttered by this unknown doctor reduced me to tears.

I still remember an unfamiliar hospice nurse putting her arms around me and telling me it was all right to let go and cry.

While I was trying to regain control of my emotions, Carolyn continued talking calmly to the doctor as if she had been informed she had a mere cold. "That doesn't surprise me," she said. "I have thought for some time that I was dying."

"If there are some things you want to do," the doctor continued, "now is the time to do them." His words were softly spoken but straight to the point.

"How long do I have?" she asked.

"Only you will know," was his evasive response.

Carolyn stopped talking, obviously thinking about what she wanted to do with the time she had left. At length, she said, "I want to see my son Scott." She paused for another breath of air. "And be around for my family reunion." Those were her only responses. She stood, and we slowly made our way back out to the car. She never shed a tear but continued on tranquilly, her faith giving her strength. That was the first lesson she taught me about dying, but it would not be her last.

During the ride home, silence enveloped us, each of us lost in the heaviness of the day. I remember thinking we ought to be talking about something—anything—because, soon, talking with one another would be taken from us. But we said nothing—that is, not until we reached the corner of our street.

"I want to go see Harry on the way home," she said abruptly.

Harry, a friend and neighbor, was also dying of cancer.

"It's been a rough day, and you are tired," I said. "Why don't we go home, put you into bed, and then call him?" But the more I persisted, the firmer became her resolve. She was going to visit Harry, and that was that.

We stopped in front of Harry's place. I helped her out of the car, carrying her oxygen tank as we slowly made our way to the front door. Her steps were measured, her breathing shallow as she stopped twice to catch her breath. Harry's wife answered the door and warmly invited us in. Carolyn laboriously made her way to Harry's darkened bedroom.

"Harry," she said between her huffs and puffs, "I just came from the doctor's office." She stopped again, struggling for breath. "He told me that I, *too*, am dying." She stressed the word *too*, letting him know that she knew he was dying, although he was in total denial.

"So," Carolyn continued, "the race is on. Whoever gets to heaven first has to greet the other with a big hug. Are we agreed?" There was no escape for Harry. She had accepted her fate. Now he needed to acknowledge and accept his. He had lived in stubborn denial for too long.

I then understood why my wife had insisted on seeing him. She wanted to help him embrace the inevitability of his condition, just as she had embraced her own. Somehow, she knew that was the only way for him to find solace and peace in dying.

That was my second lesson—and Harry's last. He passed away a few weeks later.

Our son Scott flew in from California and spent several days at his mother's bedside. At the family reunion, Carolyn's strength increased to the point where she was able to receive family members I escorted two at a time into her bedroom. There they talked, took pictures, and laughed at old times as they wandered together down memory lane. As the final two left her room, it was clear that the day's events had taken their toll. While listening to her beloved Tabernacle Choir, a choir she had sung in for many years, Carolyn fell into a deep, peaceful slumber. She died the following afternoon, still surrounded by family and friends. That was her third and final lesson for me: how to die with quiet dignity.

There was one event that took place that few witnessed but that should be mentioned because it tells how much the Lord loved Carolyn. This incident occurred as the bishop began conducting the graveside service. At that very moment, a horrible wind came up. It was so ferocious that all activities had to be suspended. Putting my mouth close to Bishop Evans' ear so he could hear me over the howling wind, I asked if he might offer a prayer that the wind would stop. The bishop put his hands out in front of him, as if to stop the wind, bowed his head, and said a silent prayer. Immediately, the wind ceased to blow, not to begin again until after the service. He later told me that he had no idea until that moment how powerful the priesthood really was. That miracle was a fitting tribute to a faithful woman.

Chapter Two

ESCAPING MY SELF-INFLICTED GRIEF

AFTER THE FUNERAL, EVERYTHING SEEMED so strange. My children went out of their way to make certain I was included in everything important in their lives. All I dwelled on was the brutal fact that every invitation was an invitation for one, not for the habitual two. There they were, my children in paired unions with their spouses and surrounded by their own children. And there I was, the only solitary adult—my presence a constant reminder that I was now somehow different.

Time seemed to drag as friends and relatives, who all had the best of intentions, dropped by with concerned advice. I listened quietly to all but paid particular attention to those who had experienced the passing of a loved one. The others didn't seem to know what they were talking about. I quickly forgave them because they didn't know that they didn't know. They were simply expressing their love for me in the only way they knew how—from their own innocent reality.

I had yet to understand my reality, however. When something seemingly out of nowhere would remind me of her passing, painful thoughts would come crashing down, cornering me into a sullen, depressed state. It only took a sad movie, an unobserved birthday, or an unplanned anniversary to set off this chain reaction. Her death was like a shadow that seemed to come and go—much like a dark cloud passing in front of the moon, allowing faint light into my life for one brief moment and then darkening it the next.

In my grief, I did not know what to do. In short, I was one of the "afflicted, tossed with tempest, and not comforted" (Isaiah 54:11). My past experiences were not particularly relevant in solving this kind of problem, nor was the counsel of my well-intentioned friends, who said such things as, "Take it one day at a time" or "This too will pass." Time seemed to change nothing for me. Like the movie *Groundhog Day*, my tomorrow was always just like my today. All I had to do was casually think about Carolyn's fight with cancer and my mind was off again, rehearsing the devastating details of her passing.

Unlike me, she had not indulged in toxic thoughts like, "What if I had discovered the cancer sooner?" or "What if I had not done the chemotherapy? How much longer would I have lived?" For her part, she entertained no such useless thoughts of blame, doubt, or despair. The past had passed. She had no anger, nor had she wasted time "bargaining" with God. She didn't have to battle any inner opposition because she had chosen to accept the reality of God's will. It seemed to me as though, by her accepting what *was*, she had somehow ignored the pain that I and others were feeling, blithely skipping through the typical stages of grief and, with unrelenting faith, quickly and quietly moved on. But how she quickly got to that last stage of acceptance was still a mystery.

In my case, the more my mind reviewed those painful events, the more confused I became. My singular grief seemed to hold no pattern or reason. Instead, I was just stuck—lost in my grief with no apparent way out.

THE TERRIBLE TRIGGER POINTS

It was about this time that I remembered what Elder Wirthlin had spoken of in one of his conference addresses. He wisely and simply said, "The way we react to adversity can be a major factor in how happy and successful we can be in life."[1] Obviously, the way I had been reacting to my adversity was not working well for me. He went on to question: "How can we love days that are filled with sorrow? We can't—at least not in the moment."

He was not suggesting that we suppress discouragement or deny the reality of pain. Nor was he suggesting that we smother unpleasant truths beneath a cloak of pretended happiness. His singular point was that how we *honestly* react to adversity can be a major factor in how happy and successful we are in life. In spite of discouragement and adversity, those who are happiest seem to have a way of learning from difficult times, becoming stronger, wiser, and happier as a result. Although I did not recognize it at the time, that also was the same "counsel" I had received from Carolyn before she passed away.

For the first time since her death many months ago, I started to examine how she had viewed her terminal condition. Up until then, I had not paid attention to the obvious: that with her own brave, faith-based example, she had already shown me the way out of my grief. For example, she had not grieved about her death sentence pronounced by some unknown doctor because she had fully accepted the conditions of that announcement. She

---

1   "Come What May, and Love It," *Ensign*, November 2008, 26.

had not entered into any second-guessing of the what-ifs of her life. She had not wallowed in the useless sorrow of things she could not change. She let all of that go. Instead, she was laser focused on the few things she wanted to do in the little time that was left: visit Harry on the way home from the hospital to help him come to terms with dying and talk to our son to help him understand what mattered most to her. After that, all she wanted to do was say good-bye to friends and family at the reunion so she could be off to visit those other friends and family waiting for her in the spirit world. She mentioned that she was particularly anxious to see her grandmother Callister—a woman she had loved dearly all of her life.

But the question remained: how was she able to ignore all of the bad things that were happening to her when many of the rest of us were thrashing about in a quagmire of grief?

While going over all of this in my mind, my thoughts led me back to the Trauma and Awareness Center and all of those patients who, like Carolyn, were able to bypass Kubler-Ross's five stages of grief. In an attempt to figure out what it was that they had done to avoid grief, I once more reviewed those stages . . . to see if I had missed something. I started with *denial*. A swift mental review led me to believe that I had no trouble with that one. I was not in denial, nor did I ever deny what was happening. That was not my problem. I quickly moved on to the second stage, *anger*. When I read that word, I was somewhat taken aback. It had not dawned on me before, but I now had to admit that not only had I been perturbed, but I was also somewhat angry—not with the cancer, as much as I hate that insidious disease, but with the doctor.

When the doctor told Carolyn she was dying, he didn't tell her the whole story. That came after she had passed away, when I telephoned him, asking for help to understand why Carolyn, who had seemed to be fairly strong before starting the chemotherapy, suddenly, in a matter of a few weeks of treatment, took a turn for the worse and died. I asked the doctor to explain how the cancer could take over so quickly, particularly when her gynecological oncologist had said her type of cancer was not that aggressive. His explanation was brief and to the point: "Oh, her cancer was not the cause of her death. She died because her body could not tolerate the chemotherapy. That is why she passed away as soon as she did."

I was dumbstruck. I could hardly believe what I had just heard. After a brief pause and while still struggling to control my emotions, I asked my next straight-to-the-point question: "If you had not administered that second round of chemotherapy," I queried, "how long would she have lived?"

"I really don't know," he responded, leaving the question hanging in midair. He didn't attempt to answer it.

But I already knew the answer . . . as did he. She would have lived *longer*! How much longer no one knows. However, one health practitioner had told us that without the debilitating effects of chemotherapy, she would probably have lived a year or more before she died. To me, a year sounded like a lifetime. What we could have done in that year!

In their wisdom, Carolyn's oncologists had reasoned that since she had cancer she was going to die anyway, so they would give her that second round of the stronger chemicals and hope for the best. If the body didn't tolerate that level of treatment, well . . . at least they had tried.

My view was different. I thought that at the very least they should have warned us of the real dangers of the more potent drug and involved us in that life-and-death decision. Now it was too late—and at this moment I had to admit that deep down there was some level of anger that had not gone away.

But I was still left with the question: how could my anger, which I did not consider to be all that detrimental, be the cause of my grief? Then, I immediately realized something that had been staring me in the face that I had not been able to see before. My anger did not have to be extraordinarily strong to cause enormous grief. It only needed to be strong enough to trigger other toxic thoughts to come forth. That's all that it would take to start an avalanche of negativity—of grief.

We all know that avalanches can sweep heavy trains off their tracks, crush buildings, uproot trees, and bury and kill people . . . but only when something or someone triggers and unleashes that horrendous power— some small factor like a single, errant skier. That was exactly what I had done with my resentment and anger. I had triggered my negative thoughts to come crashing down upon me—to bury me in a cold, debilitating grief.

Simply stated, an avalanche has three basic elements—a heavy mass of snow, a sloped surface, and a trigger. My grief also had three elements—a heavy mass of toxic thoughts (the result of my mind rehearsing over and over what had happened, causing those negative thoughts to multiply), a sloped surface (my unresolved crisis), and a trigger (my anger). To get that heavy layer of toxic ideas moving, all I needed to do was trigger them with my anger, and the whole slope of toxic thoughts would come sliding down on me. When I triggered that avalanche, I was quickly buried in my own self-imposed grief.

On the other hand, because Carolyn did not allow any negative trigger points to enter her life during those trying days, despite the devastating news that came to us both, she had no toxic thoughts to rehearse and no grief to contend with. That's what protected her. Meanwhile, I was caught up in trying to lean on my own understanding (see Prov. 3:5). I can now easily see that Carolyn found peace because she refused any damaging thoughts to steal away the precious time she had left.

I could also easily understand that there can be a variety of trigger points at every level of Kubler-Ross's five stages of grief, waiting in the shadows to set off grief in thousands of unsuspecting victims, allowing only a fortunate few to pass on unscathed to the next level. It was also clear that some trigger points could be more dangerous than others. To find out what these trigger points were, I reasoned that I would only have to analyze those who were in their grief to identify the cause.

We all have trigger points in our lives, some big and some small, that can cause endless grief if we are not careful. As a simple illustration, who would not recognize that the smell of freshly baked cookies could trigger someone to forget their diet, which could in turn make them feel and act like a failure.

Truly, trigger points come in all shapes and sizes, but they have one thing in common—they all start in the mind. And if left unrestrained, the mind can create toxic thoughts that can imprison people in a cell of self-imposed grief. That is what happened to me! That is what happens every day to thousands of others. Whatever causes your negative and toxic thoughts to come tumbling down on you is your trigger point—and it needs to be identified and, of course, controlled. At last, I had identified the why of my problem and perhaps the why of many others' problems.

While enjoying my newfound understanding, I decided to trace my thoughts back to my wife's death to see if that period had produced any good changes in my life. I began searching for some "good thoughts"—to see if they had been as helpful to me as they had been to Carolyn.

I confess, trying to find something good that had happened during those frightfully challenging times was a bit of a task. But I finally found one very positive change that had taken place. When I discovered that anger was a trigger point and how destructive it was, I no longer had a desire to judge others—doctors included. I had learned my lesson. I could now see with clarity that unrighteous judgment of others serves no real purpose. It will not change what is. I learned that, clearly, the well-known scripture, "Judge not, that ye be not judged," is more profound and meaningful than I had ever imagined (Matt. 7:1). Not only had I found one of my negative trigger points, but by realizing what it was, I was immediately able to overcome its power. My anger was gone—and so was much of my continued grief. For the first time in a long while, I had found a crack in my prison's wall.

OTHER TRIGGER POINTS

I continued on, rehearsing in my mind everything that had happened during those difficult days. But this time I was in control of my thoughts instead of them being in control of me. I excitedly traced every thought back to every response Carolyn had made when the doctor had told her she was dying. "That doesn't surprise me," she had said. "I have thought for some time that I was dying." Her accepting what *was* had to be a big clue as to why she did not end up wallowing in her self-imposed grief.

The next thing I remembered was the doctor telling Carolyn, "If there are some things you want to do, now is the time to do them." And she immediately began thinking of the things she wanted to accomplish in preparation for the next step in her journey. That *had* to be another clue. She had avoided useless thoughts of altering the past as well as any unrealistic thoughts of the future while I foolishly spent my time in the past finding fault with the doctor. With a brief smile, she had simply replied, "I want to see my son and be around for my family reunion." Then she would be ready to go. That was her final statement to the doctor.

As I rehearsed my reactions to all the events that had occurred, I found that the results were always the same. When I selected uplifting, positive thoughts based upon solid facts, I ended up with uplifting, positive feelings. The opposite was also true. When I selected negative thoughts from my anger-triggered judgment of the doctors, replaying those painful thoughts over and over in my mind, I ended up in an unhappy and painful state of mind. In every instance, I could now easily see that if I'd been more selective in my thinking, the results would have been different.

My biggest revelation was that I was indeed guilty of causing my own suffering. That understanding quickly became one of the most important "aha" moments of my life, as I hope it will be for you too. I could suddenly see very plainly that my life was the mirror image of those many case studies I had painstakingly researched. This breakthrough created another large crack in my prison wall, almost big enough to squeeze through, marking the time of my escape that much closer.

From the case studies and from my own experiences, I had brought to light many of the things we mortals do that cause us grief. With that exposure, perhaps we can learn how to avoid the terrible trigger points that always lead to grief.

Chapter Three

TRIGGER POINTS AND THE MIND'S THOUGHT SYSTEM

IN STUDYING OTHERS' GRIEF AS well as my own, I not only stumbled upon the dangers of negative trigger points and the grief they caused me and many others like me, I also quickly recognized there are positive trigger points that can also be immensely beneficial. As an illustration, think of the times you have heard something at general conference that inspired you to want to do better. (Is that not the wide-range purpose of general conference—to inspire us to be and to do better?) In addition, we have all had the experience of reading something in the scriptures (or other inspiring literature) that seemed to be penned just for us. And who can witness the birth of anything or see a beautiful sunrise or sunset and not marvel at God's creation? All of these things and many more can trigger thoughts that inspire and lift us.

The interesting thing about positive trigger points is that we don't have to wait for them to happen to us (as we too often do). We can manage our thoughts so they are always there for us whenever we want or need them. As a case in point, my patriarchal blessing instructs me to prayerfully read my blessing in times of need and that by so doing I will receive the guidance of the Holy Spirit. That blessing is always there for me.

President Packer and other General Authorities have repeatedly mentioned the power of music in keeping one's mind in tune with the Spirit. Who can hum or sing one of my favorite songs, "He That Hath Clean Hands and a Pure Heart," and trigger a bad thought? Not me. In like manner, the Brethren's counsel to read the scriptures daily is not just given for the cognitive instructive learning it provides but because it can be a primary source of spiritual growth and development.

The lesson here is that with a little planning we can refer to our preferred positive trigger points anytime we wish so that we can be stimulated to be and do better all day long. Make a mental list of the things that trigger you to be lifted up. While your favorite trigger points may be small initially, one good thought leads to another, cumulatively causing that which was triggered to assist you to grow.

Just as the tiny plant pokes its way through the earth, giving witness of the hidden seed buried therein, one's actions also give witness to the concealed seeds of thought (good or evil) buried in the recesses of the mind. Without seeing them, we know they are there because our behavior tells us so.

THE MIND'S THOUGHT SYSTEM

Since the mind is the control center of our thoughts, it is in the mind that many of our problems originate. It is in the mind that the individual is allowed to confuse the end with the means, to foster false perceptions, illusions, and delusions, as well as the fantasy of fear. As a result of man's uncontrolled mind, he can easily blacken his character while vainly attempting to polish his reputation. Each of these things is the result of the natural man's overactive mind.

From the Spirit comes one thought system, and from the natural man comes another. The first system embodies truth. It cannot exist apart from God, because all truth resides in God, and God cannot lie. The other comes from the adversary. Hence, the contamination of a man's thought system is the product and influence of the natural man, for the spirit-based man is not without his thoughts, but they are pure—they uplift, inspire, and motivate. They trigger spiritual growth and development.

Much of the natural man's thought system is found in the world of false perception. It is brought forth by the projections of the natural man and sustained by those who would follow him. This thought system is in perpetual conflict with God's because what we see and hear from the natural man often appears to be real because he permits into awareness only what conforms to the self-centered wishes of the perceiver. This leads to a world of illusions—a world that needs his constant defense precisely because it is not real. When we subscribe to the natural man, what we see merely reflects our overriding, misguided ideas and emotions.

That process is backward. We should first envision the truth and then project that onto our world, allowing that perspective to expand. If we focus on our faulty perception to justify our mistakes or focus on our anger or lack of accountability, we will see a world of iniquity, devastation, hatred, jealousy, greed, and despair. If we learn to recognize our perceptual errors, looking past them as lessons learned (not because we are being good and charitable but because what we are seeing is not true), then we can forgive others and ourselves for our distorted perceptions. At that juncture, we can easily focus on God-centered truths.

We rarely pay attention to the real power of thought itself. We simply accept it the same way we accept breathing. But the power of thought opens the door to all action, good or bad. Thoughts can even produce how we feel because thoughts and feelings are bedfellows. What you feel is the result of your thinking, not the cause of it, because what you think about is the product of what you perceive. Your outside view of yourself is an inside perception because you have nurtured it (the grass grows where it is watered). The truth remains that if you want to be a great person, you must have great thoughts. If you want to be a beautiful person, you must have beautiful thoughts. If you want to be an admirable person, you must have admirable thoughts. Thought is the guide that will take you through life exactly as you think. And as you have one good thought, it can grow as other good thoughts enter in because they are interconnected. The same logic tells us that if our thoughts get us into trouble, only our thoughts can get us out of trouble.

Thoughts are not to be accepted willy-nilly, nor do we need to be burdened, sifting through the thousands of thoughts we might have each day. Rather, we should preselect and then focus on those few core thoughts that are as close as possible to the pure intelligence that we seek—the ideas that lift us. In so doing, we allow a single, quality, laserlike thought to expand with clarity and precision, replacing the thousands of ill-considered random thoughts that we normally would have had.

It is not the number of thoughts we have that is important; rather, it is the quality of a few good thoughts that positively carry us upward that are important. As we envision the truth, we should project it forth in our thoughts and then our actions. The more we think about a particular truth, the more it expands. As we become more discriminate in our thinking, we eliminate the bad and the negative in order to use the good and the positive, stockpiling any extra for use as needed. This process is part of appropriately using our will—our agency.

President David O. McKay explained the significance of our thoughts for good or ill when he said, "The kind of life you live, your disposition, your very nature, will be determined by your thoughts, of which your acts are but the outward expression. Thought is the seed of action."[2]

---

2   *Treasures of Life*, comp. Clare M. Middlemiss (Salt Lake City, UT: Deseret Book, 1962), 200.

Like a garden, if we let our negative thoughts go unchecked, they will soon be a patch of noxious weeds—an entangling patch of pain and suffering. But if we trigger our thoughts with worthy goals, appealing to the Lord for assistance, we can succeed.

Sooner or later, we must discover that whether we harvest beautiful flowers and delicious fruit or thorny thistles and noxious briars depends on our thoughts. We are counseled to "lay hold upon every good thing" (Moro. 7:19), but we cannot do so if we dwell on only negative events, imagining potential disasters at every turn. Just as we are the gardeners of our souls, we are also the navigators of our lives. We will inevitably reap what we sow and nurture. It cannot be otherwise, for "there is a law, irrevocably decreed in heaven before the foundations of this world, upon which all blessings are predicated" (D&C 130:20). Thus we see that who we are depends on what we think—and whom we rely on.

With our thoughts, we can either lay bricks for a straight and narrow path to happiness or fashion weapons that ravage and destroy. If we wish to choose the right, we must first apply the right thoughts to the matter at hand. With the true application of charitable, optimistic thoughts, we ascend each day to become more and more like Him. Conversely, if we choose bitter, pessimistic thoughts, they will trigger us to become less and less like the Lord and more like the adversary.

During this process, we may often blame others for our miserable condition. On the other hand, we can take the opposite course. We can responsibly forge within ourselves positive thoughts that will define our good character—for those who constantly dwell in the confines of noble and lofty thoughts, who daily ponder all that is good, will surely become noble in character and happy by nature. In D&C 121:45, the Lord said, "Let virtue garnish thy thoughts unceasingly; then shall thy confidence wax strong in the presence of God."

Since our thoughts are prerequisite to our choices, carefully focusing our thoughts can be a great advantage. If we do not allow ourselves to dwell upon the unfortunate and unalterable aspects of our life (something that would do damage to mind and spirit), we will automatically eliminate much of our otherwise self-promoted grief. The Serenity Prayer explains this principle well: "God grant me the serenity to accept the things I cannot change, courage to change the things I can, and the wisdom to know the difference."[3] President Brigham Young (1801–1877) expressed

---

3   Reinhold Niebuhr, in "Origin of the Serenity Prayer: A Brief Summary," Alcoholics Anonymous, n.d., http://www.aa.org/en_pdfs/smf-141_en.pdf.

a similar, inspired philosophy: "To make ourselves happy is incorporated in the great design of man's existence. I have learned not to fret myself about that which I cannot help. If I can do good, I will do it; and if I cannot reach a thing, I will content myself to be without it. This makes me happy all the day long."[4]

Like many others, I had to learn the hard way that if we listen long enough to our negative thoughts, we soon behave as if we *are* our thoughts. Logic tells us that we need to control them so they do not control us. If we do not, we can end up the same way that I and countless others did—in overwhelming grief. We need to select those thoughts that will allow us to ride out of our grief, not be "saddled" with it.

Thinking is like breathing. For the most part, it is involuntary and repetitive. Depending on what is being considered, it can also be dangerous. Rarely do any of us control what we think about when not engaged in a specific task. We simply let our minds wander, live in some wild fantasy, or retrieve a sad memory. Our thoughts often become, as it were, free agents who do as they please. Obviously, not being able to stop our negative, incessant thoughts can be a terrible affliction.

Because nearly everyone is subject to letting his or her thoughts run wild, we tend to think it is just the way life is. But, clearly, that is not so. For example, children's innocent minds typically think in the present moment, not in the past, as they create events for their play. As adults, however, we seem to spend much of our time rehearsing past memories, often causing us to create false labels, critical judgments of others, and erroneous beliefs.

The conscious mind carries out the responsibility of choice. It reasons, deduces, judges, discriminates, influences, and generally gives direction as to how we are to live. In its normal routine of deciding what to think, the mind often conjures events and people to worry about, things to fear, and visions of poverty, disharmony, and grief. But if so directed, it also has the capacity to present the other side of the "coin," as previously mentioned.

A runaway mind can falsely justify the means with the end, foster fake perceptions, and create illusions and fantasies of fear. In our minds, what we often hear appears to be real because it conforms with our desires or fears. This leads to a fantasy world—a world that needs the natural man's constant attention precisely because it is not real. In this fantasy world, thoughts and feelings are inseparably linked. You can't have a good feeling with a bad thought, nor can you have a bad feeling with a good thought. That singular fact speaks volumes.

---

4   *Journal of Discourses*, 2:95.

Of course, as we entertain one thought, similar thoughts are fostered. (One thought always leads to another.) But it is for us to instruct the mind as to what that first thought should be so it can grow in strength and purpose as other supporting thoughts appear. Once we have learned this important lesson, we have understanding. With that understanding, we gain maturity. With the strength of maturity, we can alter our self-defeating patterns, never underestimating our power when combined with the power and mercy of the Lord. Each of us can literally become what we think. Proverbs 23:7 proclaims, "For as he thinketh in his heart, so is he." Or, to quote a favorite saying of President David O. McKay: "We sow our thoughts, and we reap our actions; we sow our actions, and we reap our habits; we sow our habits, and we reap our characters; we sow our characters, and we reap our destiny."[5]

---

5   C. A. Hall, *The Home Book of Quotations* (New York: Dodd, Mead & Company, 1935), 845.

Chapter Four

HOW TO CONTROL A NEGATIVE MIND

BUT THE QUESTION STILL REMAINS: how do you control negative thinking that seems to continually bombard your peace of mind? To accomplish that task, think of walking down a road with a chatty friend. You listen attentively to what he says, quietly discriminating the worth of his comments. But you never think for one instant that you are your friend. That would be absurd. Now, think of walking down the same road with your mind somehow walking beside you and telling you all kinds of things. Just as you did while walking with your friend, you quietly discriminate the worth of the thoughts from your own mind, keeping those that lift and inspire while discarding the others. But never think for one instant that you are irreversibly defined by your thoughts any more than you would think that you are irreversibly defined by who your friends are. But that's the beauty of it! We can control who we are by controlling what we think of who we are. To illustrate this point, let me tell you about the experience of a man I will call Michael.

Michael was active in his ward and community. He worked as an accountant for a rather large firm in the city. He and his wife raised a family of four boys. But not long after the children arrived, his wife started showing signs of a serious health problem. All the joints in her body seemed to ache. While it didn't take long for the doctors to identify the problem, they were never able to cure her of that serious arthritic disease. From that time on, she lived in constant pain, and Michael became her constant support and caregiver.

Through the years, their lives became increasingly difficult. Michael valiantly continued caring for her: bathing her, taking her to the bathroom, dressing her, and fixing her meals. She often mentioned how loving and kind he was to her, how he never voiced a complaint. To the contrary, as she continually became more frail, his love and dedication for her seemed to increase. Finally—and mercifully—she passed away. Since my wife too had also passed away, Michael and I had something in common—something that bonded us as nothing else could or would. When his wife died, I immediately went to see him. That was the beginning of many visits and long discussions.

On those occasions, he did most of the talking and I the listening. He could not get over the death of his wife. He had adored her, always believing that he had married above himself. With every visit, I saw him grow more sullen. He talked endlessly about what a saint his wife had been—and how he hadn't deserved her. The more he remembered her life, the more his thoughts told him how unworthy he was of her love. Though I offered him constant reminders of his own many virtues and the contributions he had made in the community and as a caregiver, he seemed oblivious to any of my comments. His unresponsiveness continued until he finally fell into a deep depression. After watching weeks of his self-torture, his family came to me for help. I quickly found a competent therapist for him who, little by little, was able to bring him back to reality and to safety.

His problem was simple (or so said the therapist). Michael's thoughts of his wife focused on everything that was good about her (which was easy to do because she was an exceptional woman), and everything that was, in his mind, bad about himself. Instead of basking in the memory of the many good times they had spent together or how he had served her in sickness and health, he let his corrosive thoughts expand. Those thoughts convinced him that since he could never be as good as his spouse, he was of little use to anyone. Instead of controlling his misguided thoughts, his thoughts began controlling him. Finally, all of his pain triggered an artificial reality, and he slipped into a painful, illusionary world. He *became* who his misguided thoughts said he was.

Because Michael believed he was who his thoughts made him out to be, he could not let go of those harmful beliefs, fearing that by so doing he would be letting go of himself. But the contrary was actually true. As he scraped away those self-deprecating thoughts, he was not discarding himself but rather discarding what had placed him in bondage. He thus regained control over his life by developing the power to control his thoughts. A year later, he found and married another marvelous lady.

To better understand Michael's condition, think of how our thoughts often erroneously define who we are: "I am a farmer," "I am a musician," "I am a housewife," "I am a teacher." Of course, we may *do* what is required to fulfill these vocations, but we are *not* our jobs. Others may negatively define themselves as fat or skinny, tall or short, but that isn't who they are either. They are not their bodies. Then there are those who negatively define themselves as worthless or by any number of other self-destructive definitions. But those definitions are not who they are. We must recognize that these negative thoughts are ill-conceived notions that feed off the negativity they generate.

I vividly remember one evening during the 2002 Salt Lake City Winter Olympics that dramatically demonstrates this point. I had left my hotel and was walking the downtown streets of Salt Lake. The city lights were ablaze, and the sounds of music and happy people were everywhere—everywhere, that is, except on the corner of Main Street and South Temple. There, in the midst of all the gaiety was a dirty, shabbily dressed man shouting obscenities to no one in particular. His ranting caused more than one passerby to stop and stare and then take a wide detour around him. A lady just in front of me tightened her grip on her child's hand as she leaned over to dispatch a warning in the child's ear. "Don't get too close to him, honey," I heard her say. "He's crazy." Crazy or not, I could not judge. What I *could* see was a poor man loudly responding to a voice in his head that told him exactly what to say and what to do.

What is the difference between that babbling person on the street and us? Don't we also listen to and obey or battle the sometimes uncontrolled inner voice that speaks to us? Just because we don't respond out loud to what that inner voice is saying, as he did, does not classify us as normal and him as crazy. The determining factor of our mental (and spiritual health) lies in our ability to quiet the mind, to have it work for us and not be obligated to obey it.

But how do we do that? Well, let's assume you are going on a walk. On that walk, take with you a pad and pencil. As you walk, don't try to control your thoughts—just let them go wherever they want to go in a stream of consciousness. As you listen to them, make a note of each: "Today during my walk, I first thought about _____, then I thought about _____." By the time you return from your short walk, you will have made several notations about your thoughts. Later, review and organize your notes into different categories and ask yourself, "How profitable were my thoughts today? Was I uplifted or edified? Did I solve a particular problem?" Those who have tried this simple exercise have found that their random thoughts, with rare exception, led nowhere. They were as a ship without a rudder, drifting aimlessly on the sea of life, constantly reviewing the memories stored up in their minds. You too may come to the same conclusion.

Now, let's assume you take another walk, but this time you write down what you want your mind to think about beforehand, making certain these "trigger" items are important to you. Then, as you walk, you let your mind consider each of those items . . . and nothing else. At the end of your walk, again ask yourself, "How profitable were my thoughts for me today? Was I uplifted and edified, or did I solve a particular problem?" As you compare the two different walk experiences, you will easily see which one worked best for you. When set to an actual task, your mind is much more likely to produce edifying solutions to your problems and to employ uplifting strategies that will help you obtain your worthy goals. You may be surprised to know that much of this book was organized and refined on my morning walks.

You may note that the important goals and issues your mind considered during your second walk led to generating useful strategies and solutions in a relatively short period of time. What if your mind were constantly busy constructing, analyzing, synthesizing, and creating such thoughts throughout the day, not just during the few minutes of a walk? What might take place if you consistently selected and prioritized your thoughts? This process easily explains why some people are more productive than others.

Ideally, you should have a genuine purpose in your heart and ponder that purpose every day. That would serve as your positive trigger point. Those who do not have a central purpose in mind might well begin by focusing their thoughts on how they perform responsibilities, regardless of how insignificant those tasks may appear. When your performance is improved in even these seemingly insignificant tasks, as it surely will be, you will be motivated to achieve even loftier goals. Thus we see that the task is not just in achieving something but also in learning how to achieve. Remember that the great oak was once asleep in the acorn. Dreams are the seedlings of miracles. Focused thoughts reveal the path to achievement.

Pondering a laudable purpose is akin to offering a secret prayer, particularly if the purpose is Godlike in nature. It may surprise you how quickly inspiration will come to you when your central purpose mirrors God's central purpose. As the Prophet Joseph Smith learned in a miraculous event we know as the First Vision, the Lord promises us: "If any of you lack wisdom, let him ask of God, that giveth to all men liberally, and upbraideth not; and it shall be given him" (James 1:5). The Lord declared this same promise with variations in Luke 11:9: "And I say unto you, Ask, and it shall be given you; seek, and ye shall find; knock, and it shall be opened unto you."[6]

When the mind is focused, it produces. To be efficient is to give the mind direction as to what it is to do. Obviously, that is the path successful

---

6   See also 1 Chr. 28:9; Luke 11:9; 3 Ne. 14:7; D&C 18:18; 88:63–64; Abr. 2:12.

people have taken to reach their dreams. Identify your dream and focus on that dream day in and day out. You will be amazed at how absolutely brilliant and productive you are when your thoughts are focused and linked to a special purpose. One of the great residual benefits that results from this exercise is the self-confidence generated when you recognize that, with divine guidance, you can achieve the righteous desires of your heart (if, indeed, it is in your best interests). In D&C 88:64, Christ declared, "Whatsoever ye ask the Father in my name it shall be given unto you, *that is expedient for you*" (emphasis added).

As you listen to the thoughts in your head, pay particular attention to repetitive ideas that may have been sounding off for years. If those thoughts are the offspring of some sad event that you can do nothing about, simply refuse to allow the mind to "talk" about how unfair it was or how your life would be different without that experience. When your mind generates a thought that is not accurate or beneficial, particularly a recurring thought you confronted and disproved long ago, simply quit listening. That leaves your mind with nothing to say—at least about that toxic subject.

If you're unsure how to do this, begin by running through a series of probing questions.[7] When you find yourself in a bad mood, search for a triggering event and the thoughts that contributed to that troubled mood. Begin by identifying the worst habitual thought(s) or belief(s) you have conjured up about yourself. Then search for evidence that *opposes* those chronically negative thoughts. Armed with your new evidence, you are now in a position to come up with more positive, balanced beliefs or thoughts about yourself and your situation. Now, as you take stock of your current mood, do you feel any better? More clearheaded and hopeful? It is through this process that you can choose thoughts that have lasting, constructive value and not be tricked into accepting thoughts that are, by their nature, paralyzing and useless. We can remain miserable by refusing to change our thoughts, or we can find peace by elevating our thoughts out of the abyss of our problems. Within this simple concept lies the key to happiness.

Much has been said about the terrible things that can result from negative trigger points that allow the mind to run wild, creating additional negative,

---

7   With the exception of involving prayer and other spiritual practices, the following steps of Cognitive Behavioral Therapy (CBT) are described in much more depth by Dr. Dennis Greenberger and Dr. Christine A. Padesky in their book, *Mind Over Mood: Change How You Feel by Changing the Way You Think* (New York: Guilford Press, 1995).

linking thoughts that build on each other and seem to go on forever. In my case, I could have overridden those negative trigger points that caused so much grief had I just focused on the positive trigger points all around me. That is what Carolyn did, and by so doing, she was oblivious to all of the negative thoughts besieging me. If we become proactive—replacing negative with positive trigger points in every aspect of our lives—we can expect to be free of any self-generated grief. If we try to always focus on positive trigger points, self-defeating thoughts will have little chance to influence our actions, thus keeping us safe from personal harm.

Seeking positive trigger points will not only protect you but will also make you happy. Daily seeking inspiration and personal revelation through study, pondering, and prayer will keep negative trigger points at bay. One of the things that makes me immensely happy is when I feel spiritually inspired. When that happens, I know I am loved. I feel a great sense of gratitude, and my prayers reflect the same. I feel at one with my Heavenly Father as well as with the universe. Those thoughts are some of my positive trigger points. You will find that as you open your mind to inspiration and let the Lord guide you, it will become filled with thoughts that will lead you in a positive direction where you will find true happiness and fulfillment. Remember, the Lord intends for us to be happy (see 2 Ne. 2:25), so we are wise when we allow Him to guide our thinking.

As a former mission president, I learned much of what I know about personal inspiration and revelation from my missionaries. In particular, I remember two sister missionaries who were sent to reopen an area that had previously been closed because of inactivity. That area had been called "Mission Impossible." Within two months, those two sister missionaries were baptizing families. When I asked them what they were doing to find so many of the Lord's elect, particularly in that previously barren area, they said, "President, when we moved into the area, we started our work with fasting and daily prayer, asking the Lord to show us His will. Within days, we knew what we were to pray for—how the Lord wanted us to proceed—and within two weeks, we had put into practice His plan. Then everything just worked fine. We didn't really do anything. The Lord did it all."

It didn't surprise me that these two missionaries began their work with a special fast. What did surprise me was they fasted and prayed *to know what the Lord wanted*, not what they wanted. I suspect that most missionaries would have prayed that they might be successful and then gone about their labors, just as they had always done. However, the sisters didn't do as they had always done. They stopped that old process to find out what the Lord would have them do. Within a short time, their prayers had been answered. A new approach to finding the Lord's elect had been revealed to them.

The Lord's plan was totally different from what I had developed for the mission and different from what other missionaries were doing. But it was the Lord's way, not theirs. As a point of interest, we later adopted that plan for the entire mission, and the mission quickly doubled its baptisms.

President Spencer W. Kimball fasted and prayed to know the Lord's will regarding all worthy males holding the priesthood. He not only fasted and prayed but also went to the temple every week for a number of years before the Lord revealed His plan. President Kimball was obviously opening his mind to the things the Lord would have him think and do. And when it was finally revealed—the Lord's plan, not President Kimball's—it greatly increased the number of worthy people coming into the Church.

What I learned from my two missionaries was the importance of finding what out what the Lord wants through personal inspiration or revelation so that we may accomplish His desires. Focusing on serving the Lord and doing His will creates a solid foundation for success and happiness, as my young missionaries taught me.

Chapter Five

BE PRESENT

As I became more and more aware of the need to think thoughts that would lift me out of my grief, I was surprised how little of that I had done in the past. How many times during the day do you conscientiously instruct your mind what to think about? Not all that often, I would guess. Of course, when the mind functions without you being "present," so to speak, you forfeit your right to choose what you think about. It literally chooses for you. Consider that when a crisis enters one's life, that trauma creates a great opportunity for the mind to review it over and over. Often, we not only let that happen but even encourage it. What good is it to review such disastrous events over and over, as I did when my wife died? Would it not serve you better to allow your negative thoughts to retreat and get some balance back in your life?

Allowing our thoughts to choose the direction of our lives without understanding where that choice will lead is problematic at best and life threatening at worst. If we allow our misguided thoughts to become the driving force in our lives, we can ultimately find ourselves being driven by them. How many times have you been traveling along the freeway, thinking of anything but what you are experiencing in the present moment, when suddenly you realize you have been on mental "cruise control" for the last five or ten minutes? When that happens, you are totally oblivious to anything that transpired while you were lost in random and probably insignificant thoughts. You could have focused on God's wonders and creations just outside your window. You could have considered a meaningful memory or mentally solved a problem. You missed these opportunities and many others like them because you were not present to direct your mind to engage in more productive and happy considerations.

Additionally, we not only have to keep in touch with our present physical reality, we also have to be in touch with our present spiritual reality. If we aren't in tune with the Spirit, we may not receive important personal inspiration. We must always guard against any interference the adversary may wish to inflict upon us.

President Boyd K. Packer talked of the importance of filtering out unwanted interference, particularly that which sometimes occurs when we pray. He told of how his son, who had always been interested in radio, could talk with someone in a distant part of the world and filter out interference that others could not. President Packer's point was that we too need to separate out all of the confusion that comes to us if we are to hear the quiet voice of inspiration.[8]

Just as President Packer's son was able to attune his listening ear to what was being said to him, we must also learn to attune our listening ear to the things God would say to us—to those things that matter most. We too often tune in to our past mistakes or thoughts of what we would do if we had this or that. By so doing, we miss what is happening right now.

You cannot be happy in the past or the future, for happiness exists only in the present. Therefore it is important to become aware of what is happening right now, for only in the present can you direct your mind to select thoughts that will lead to your desired outcome—your happiness. The degree to which you are present—or how consistently you refuse to allow your thoughts to take you on some meaningless, unauthorized excursion to the past or into the future—is the degree to which you control your destiny.

When you are not actively controlling your mind, your thoughts will present the story of your life as if you were that story. But you are not the story of your life. All the things that happened to you were just events in your life. Those trials and triumphs helped shape you, but those events are not you.

In one of our weekly sessions, Dr. Beall once reviewed with me the case study of a female patient who turned her husband's innocuous behavior into evidence of his supposed unfaithfulness. She first became irate with her husband when she saw him innocently chewing gum (her ex-husband used to do so in order to freshen his breath before he left to see another woman). Her uncontrolled thoughts automatically told her that her second husband must be chewing gum for the same reason. When confronted, her husband tried to defend himself, but she would not listen. The more he protested, the more convinced she was of his guilt and the more upset and hurt she became. Perceiving her husband to be the cause of her pain, she cried in her mind, *You can't trust any man to be faithful.*

---

8   "Prayers and Answers," *Ensign*, November 1979, 19.

Her savage attack against her husband was simply an expression of her renewed pain. Her past hurtful memories automatically caused an erroneous judgment of her current husband's behavior. That, in turn, triggered an emotionally charged response that allowed her excruciating past experiences to completely overcome her. She first became suspicious, then irate, and, at length, totally irrational as she used her false logic to justify her condemning words. But that enraged person wasn't who she was—she had simply allowed her thoughts of a past betrayal to direct and control her actions.

Her unchecked thoughts created her negative emotions, and those negative emotions "confirmed" that her automatic thoughts were real. Obviously, this is a case of flawed circular logic. Yet this all took place when her thoughts told her that she was again reliving a story from her life—one in which she was the victim of a cheating husband. Had she learned not to associate painful memories with present events, but rather to simply live in the present with a husband who truly loved her, she would have been happy.

While the resolution to her problem was not that easy to come by, it is evident that at the very least, she should have put an expiration date on all of the bad things her past abusive ex-husband had done to her and thrown those thoughts away as quickly as she would throw away a smelly carton of milk after its expiration date. Sour thoughts, like sour milk, should be immediately tossed out.

Unfortunately, forgiving others and overcoming pain is not as easy as throwing out an old carton of milk. Our minds are masters of creating connections. Sadly, they sometimes make poor connections, as was the case with this woman whose first husband was unfaithful. But with patience and practice, we can learn to direct our thoughts to deal with grief in productive ways. As President Kimball once proclaimed, "Suffering can make saints of people as they learn patience, long-suffering, and self-mastery."[9]

No one necessarily wants to grieve, and yet evidence confirms that many of us cause ourselves unnecessary grief—and we seem to do it well. Take a moment to think of how someone mistreated you, cheated you, lied to you, stole from you, took advantage of you, spoke badly of you, or any other toxic event you might have in your memory bank. Were it not for the Atonement, you would probably have a difficult time recalling such an event without inviting depression. We must be vigilant in recognizing what unchecked toxic thoughts can do to us. By so doing we can overcome any unresolved grief and break down larger patterns of grief-provoking thoughts.

---

9   *Faith Precedes the Miracle* (Salt Lake City, UT: Deseret Book, 1972), 98.

I will venture a guess that some of you currently have some unresolved grief in your life—grief that probably continues to plague you because you are not controlling the "automatic" thoughts that cause your grief. I remember that until I experienced that kind of grief, I was totally oblivious to such a possibility. I would never have believed that I could be causing my own grief. I now understand how living in that "unconscious" state allowed my unchallenged thoughts to repeat themselves over and over, shrouding me in a cloud of darkness. But here is the good news: as soon as I became *aware* that such was the case, the pain stopped.

Stop thinking about your past heartaches and grief as if they will happen again. Recognize those memories for what they are—negative thoughts of events that exist *only* in the past. Exchange them for present thoughts that are uplifting and meaningful to you. Think of the beautiful things you might be seeing, hearing, smelling, and feeling right now in this very moment. Then you can begin challenging the "truths" hidden in your negative thoughts— the lies that *seem* like truths because such thoughts have plagued you for so long. Put a conclusion on such thoughts and move on.

After Carolyn passed away and I finally overcame my grief, I eventually found a wonderful woman and married again. As my new wife, Rena, and I began to make a life together, we decided to move to a new community where we could build our dream home. We found a talented architect and a contractor and began our project. In that process, we conscientiously selected the very best materials for our home, as well as the very best furnishings that we could find within our budget. With time, our efforts paid off. We ended up with a beautiful home we loved.

We might compare building and furnishing such a new home to the "home" we build in our minds—the one furnished with life's lessons. Should we not be as conscientious in the selection of the thoughts and memories we choose to furnish our minds with as we are of the furnishings we put into a home? Should we carelessly allow grief or feelings of hate to be the cornerstones of our home?

Wherever we live, we must take out the garbage, clean the rooms, and routinely take care of any needed maintenance if we want to have welcoming, orderly homes. In like manner, should we not take out the garbage, clean the "rooms," and perform any necessary maintenance of our minds? Should we build special "guest rooms" for the memories of this man or that woman who offended or took advantage or us or for the painful mistakes we have made? Do we really want a noisy "houseguest" to stay on forever so as to always remind us of those hurtful memories? When considered in this light, the scenario is ridiculous, although it would seem that many of us are trapped in it all the same.

Some of you may even purposefully bludgeon yourself with negative thoughts of your mistakes, thinking that you *deserve* to feel such unending pain. But such thoughts are actually in direct opposition to the gospel's teaching. Godly sorrow for our sins is requisite for repentance, but if we wallow in self-pitying sorrow, we are effectively shunning the great sacrifice that Christ made for us in the Garden of Gethsemane and on the cross. As we read in Doctrine and Covenants 88:33, "For what doth it profit a man if a gift is bestowed upon him, and he receive not the gift? Behold, he rejoices not in that which is given unto him, neither rejoices in him who is the giver of the gift."

Stop and examine the memories you've stored in your "home." As you do so, you may be surprised to find that not only have you built a special guest room for your existing grief, but you also invite your gloomy houseguest to come out of his room to visit with you—to tell his hurtful tales over and over. How tragic is that? How could you ever be free of your grief under such circumstances? How could you ever expect to have peace in your life living that way? Instead of inviting such a destructive houseguest into our minds, we must seek to invite the Savior and the healing power of the Atonement into our hearts and minds, for He has said, "Behold, I stand at the door, and knock" (Rev. 3:20). All we need to do is to invite Him in. It makes sense.

COMMON SENSE

Being present is more than just a tool for screening out bad memories and selecting the good. It is the basis for making wise decisions—decisions that often only require the application of some common gospel sense. One example of good old common sense is contained in the Word of Wisdom (see D&C 89). In that revelation, the Lord simply told us that tobacco is not good for the body. However, many people still smoke, often becoming addicted. Common sense also tells them that smoking can be injurious to their health, but too often these people are simply on "automatic response." Without thinking, they light up without really being "present." The global result is that thousands of smokers die painful deaths each year.

Common sense tells us that all of our "automatic" thoughts should not be accepted willy-nilly, nor should all of our spontaneous decisions be acted upon. Benjamin Franklin was right: "An ounce of prevention is worth a pound of cure."[10]

Without common sense we would be weighed down by the added burden of sifting through the thousands of thoughts we might have each day. We should use regular scripture study and sincere prayer to preselect and then efficiently focus on core goals and beliefs that are as close as possible to the direction and intelligence we seek. By so doing, we encourage a worthwhile thought, with laserlike focus, to expand with clarity and precision, replacing the multitude of ill-considered, random thoughts we normally might have had. We must first envision our desires and then project them forth through our thoughts and our actions.

Elder M. Russell Ballard taught that we need common sense more than ever in today's world.[11] The lack thereof, he pointed out, is often the source of much unnecessary hardship. To illustrate this point, he related an old anecdote about a pharmacist who needed to grind enough strychnine, a fatal chemical when administered in high does, to cover a dime for a particular prescription. But, not having a dime, he used two nickels instead! Clearly, two nickels add up to a dime in monetary value but *not* in surface area. One can only hope that the pharmacist discovered his mistake before the customer came for the medicine.

In the same article, Elder Ballard also quoted Lord Chesterfield, the British statesman and orator, who observed, "Common sense (which, in truth, is very uncommon) is the best sense I know of: abide by it; it will counsel you best."[12] Unsurprisingly, Elder Ballard noted that part of common sense or "thinking straight," as he put it, is learning to seek the Lord's will and obey the whisperings of the Spirit. The Lord has promised much if we do so: "For by my Spirit will I enlighten them, and by my power will I make known unto them the secrets of my will—yea, even those things which eye has not seen, nor ear heard, nor yet entered into the heart of man" (D&C 76:10). Consequently, the more we are present in the now to think about a particular, righteous desire, the more it will expand. As we learn to discriminate among our thoughts, we can eliminate

---

10   "Franklin's Philadelphia: Fire Department," The Electric Benjamin Franklin, n.d., http://www.ushistory.org/franklin/philadelphia/fire.htm. This was quoted in a letter Franklin wrote to the *Pennsylvania Gazette*, dated February 4, 1735.

11   "Becoming Self-Reliant Spiritually and Physically," *Ensign*, March 2009, 50–55.

12   From *A New Dictionary of Quotations on Historical Principles*, sel. and ed. H. L. Mencken (New York: Alfred Knopf, 1976), 1084.

the negative, false, and useless ones and replace them with positive, true, and productive thoughts.

As you read these comments and guidelines, see if, in your own mind, these things make sense or not. If they do, apply them to your life. If they don't, forget them. That is the only test you need to apply.

WHAT YOU THINK IS WHAT YOU BELIEVE

One hurdle in overcoming grief is the way distorted thoughts often create a powerful illusion of truth. These thoughts "feel" right because the thoughts you habitually think are what you come to believe. Since what's in your mind feeds your feelings, the distance between what you feel and what is truth can be ever increasing, particularly when your thoughts are shrouded in grief.

Let's compare emotional pain with the physical pain you would experience from a broken arm. You may know what you must do to fix your broken arm, but often, you may not know how to fix your "broken" emotions, your ever-present grief, because you fail to realize that how you *feel* is most often the result of how and what you *think*. Without that understanding, anyone would be at a loss as to what to do.

Think about those key quality thoughts that can give you "upward" mobility in this present moment. Then project them forth in your thoughts and actions. Make both a "to-be" and a "to-do" list because you should set a goal to be able to answer these straightforward questions with some measure of assurance: "What will I be today?" and "What will I do for myself and others today?" The answers to those questions will reveal your discriminating choices and your discriminating thoughts. Focusing on these goals will allow you to quiet your mind by not allowing entrance to extraneous, ill-advised, or distorted thoughts. With practice and the Lord's guidance, you will then be able to answer the larger question of who you really are.

Christ admonished us to become as a little child, "submissive, meek, humble, patient, full of love, willing to submit to all things which the Lord seeth fit to inflict upon him, even as a child doth submit to his father" (Mosiah 3:19). This is a great model, for, in general, children are quick to forgive and forget. The minds of little children allow them to find joy in the present moment, for that is where they find their happiness. Their thoughts are not often occupied with the past. Except in cases of chronic child abuse, children tend not to rehearse their grief over and over in their minds.

In his popular book, *The Mastery of Love*, Don Miguel Ruiz illustrated this principle: "If you see two children playing together, and they start to fight and hit each other, the children cry and run to their mothers. 'Hey, she hit me!' One mother goes to talk to the other mother. The two mothers have a big fight, and five minutes later the two children again are playing together as if nothing happened. Now the mothers hate each other for the rest of their lives."[13]

Once again, think of the times you have felt offended, misjudged, or ill-treated by someone because you let oppressive thoughts come tumbling down on you. As you rehearsed those past events in your mind, your so-called problems grew more and more daunting because what you focus on always expands. But if we don't focus obsessively on what others have said or done to us or where we have gone wrong ourselves, we no longer create seemingly insurmountable problems. If we have no supposedly unfixable problems, we have no unconquerable grief. If we have no grief that cannot be healed, we can become the recipients of the other side of grief—happiness and peace to our souls.

It is vital that we learn to be present in the now, to "let virtue continually garnish [our] thoughts unceasingly" (D&C 121:45). In his small but famous book, *As a Man Thinketh*, James Allen describes the power of virtuous thought:

> Beautiful thoughts of all kinds crystallize into habits of grace and kindliness, which solidify into genial and sunny circumstances: pure thoughts crystallize into habits of temperance and self-control, which solidify into circumstances of repose and peace: thoughts of courage, self-reliance, and decision crystallize into manly habits, which solidify into circumstances of success, plenty, and freedom: energetic thoughts crystallize into habits of cleanliness and industry, which solidify into circumstances of pleasantness: gentle and forgiving thoughts crystallize into habits of gentleness, which solidify into protective and preservative circumstances: loving and unselfish thoughts crystallize into habits of self-forgetfulness for others, which solidify into circumstances of sure and abiding prosperity and true riches.[14]

True riches are often the result of instructing the mind on what to think about, not allowing it to decide. True riches often occur when we are in tune

---

13   *The Mastery of Love* (San Rafael, CA: Amber-Allen Publishing, 1999), 172.

14   *As a Man Thinketh* (New York: Cosimo, 2010), 28.

with the Spirit and do not allow static and interference from the adversary to govern our minds. True riches are ours when we keep our minds free of toxic thoughts. Those need to be turned over to the Lord, trusting in His promise that He will resolve our problems in His own due time (see D&C 121:7, 8).

Chapter Six

JUDGMENT

EVERY TIME I LOOK AT the lists of triggers that help create a person's self-imposed grief, I am amazed by the number of dangerous practices found therein. They generally point not to some relatively unknown or hidden secret but to things that are often so common that they almost go unnoticed. Unwarranted judgment is one of these.

We have been warned many times of the dangers of being judgmental of others and, as a matter of fact, of being judgmental of ourselves. "Judge not, that ye be not judged" is one of those commonly known scriptures that too often seems to just "hover in the air," never seriously entering our hearts and minds. Somehow we need to recognize the true import of the Lord's admonition and do something about it. But we tend to judge so automatically that it can almost be considered the "right" thing to do. I will use my own experience—my own moment of weakness—to illustrate.

Some years ago, my wife and I volunteered to serve in a well-known humanitarian program in South America. We enjoyed everything about that experience except for the chief administrator. To me, it seemed as if his actions were often based on selfish interests and that those interests had a debilitating effect on the overall program. I finally wrote him a disparaging letter with the evidence I had laboriously compiled to prove that he had succumbed to feelings of entitlement while acting in his "lofty" position—and to point out all of the mistakes he had made as a result. I told myself I needed to write that letter so as to help him, as well as the rest of us who were subject to his self-centered decisions.

As I pondered my well-documented letter, I felt an uneasiness creep into my being. As I reread my words, I became aware that in my zeal to point out his errors, I had disqualified all of the good things this man had accomplished and undoubtedly would continue to accomplish. I had singled out a few of his negative traits and behaviors, reducing everything he had done to these negative impressions. In the language of psychologists, dismissing all the favorable aspects of a person or event by focusing on one (supposedly) negative aspect is called "selective abstraction." Those judgmental thoughts I selected grew and grew in my mind because they were all I focused on. Once a higher source of inspiration helped me realize what I had been doing, I turned my attention to all the good he had done. After that, the administrator's errors did not seem anywhere near as glaring, and my discontent was simply snuffed out. He probably never even realized that some of us were displeased.

Selective abstraction can quickly escalate to dangerous proportions in relationships that are more intimate. For example, how many marriages have been strained or broken because the wife or the husband (or both) picked out a real or perceived flaw in the other and focused on that single issue? Selective abstraction can quickly cause the faultfinder to disqualify all the good qualities in his or her mate, leaving only the perceived flaw. Its lethal power can appear so innocent that it is easy to ignore it. Lola B. Walters' story in the April 1993 *Ensign* illustrates this principle. She said she had been married about two years when she read a magazine article recommending that married couples regularly discuss, truthfully and candidly, the habits or mannerisms they found annoying in each other. The theory was that if the partners knew of such annoyances, they could correct them before resentful feelings developed. She talked to her husband about it, and after some time, he agreed to give it a try. This is what she said of that experience:

> As I recall, we were to name five things we found annoying, and I started off. After more than 50 years, I remember only my first complaint: grapefruit. I told him that I didn't like the way he ate grapefruit. He peeled it and ate it like an orange! Nobody else I knew ate grapefruit like that. Could a girl be expected to spend a lifetime, and even eternity, watching her husband eat grapefruit like an orange? Although I have forgotten them, I'm sure the rest of my complaints were similar.
>
> After I finished, it was his turn to tell the things he disliked about me. Though it has been more than half a century, I still carry a mental image of my husband's handsome young face as he gathered his brows together in a thoughtful, puzzled frown and then looked at me with

his large blue-gray eyes and said, "Well, to tell the truth, I can't think of anything I don't like about you, Honey." . . .

I wish I could say that this experience completely cured me of fault finding. It didn't. But it did make me aware early in my marriage that husbands and wives need to keep in perspective, and usually ignore, the small differences in their habits and personalities. Whenever I hear of married couples being incompatible, I always wonder if they are suffering from what I now call the Grapefruit Syndrome.[15]

Selective abstractions do not take place just between husbands and wives. There are other forms of the same malady—such as when we "disqualify" ourselves or when we dismiss our actual accomplishments. Anytime you exclusively focus on your own shortcomings, you will probably end up telling yourself, *This proves what I've known all along. I'm no good.* In like manner, if you accomplish something outstanding, you might say to yourself, *That was just a fluke. It doesn't count.* Don't disqualify the truth. Recognize that "cognitive distortion" (another term the psychologists use when one distorts the truth) is commonplace and is often what forms the basis for serious depression. Don't let your distorted thoughts take you there.

The truth is that we are mortal and we make mistakes. We then repent and try again. But if we allow ourselves to believe we are *no good*, we have missed the power of the Atonement. When we stop judging our own inabilities and simply turn inward, so to speak, we are no longer encumbered by compulsive, competitive comparisons with others whose talents may overshadow our own. We should simply open our ears and listen to what our all-knowing, all-powerful Father in Heaven would have us do with our talents, regardless of how the world favors certain abilities over others. And when we seek to turn our weaknesses into strengths, we must be willing to offer up "a broken heart and contrite spirit" to the Lord (3 Ne. 9:20).

Consider that for every negative judgment you make, you can probably find ten positive things that could be said—both of yourself and others. When you're tempted to focus on someone's flaws, you may want to remember this commandment—"Judge not, and ye shall not be judged: condemn not, and ye shall not be condemned: forgive, and ye shall be forgiven" (Luke 6:37).

Consider too that you many have completely misjudged someone else's actions or words. On this subject, President N. Eldon Tanner had this comment:

---

15 "The Grapefruit Syndrome," *Ensign*, April 1993, 13.

There is a little story about Sister McKay, the wife of President David O. McKay, when she began teaching school. As the principal introduced her to the class, he pointed to a certain boy and said he was a troublemaker. She sensed the boy's embarrassment and feared he would live up to his reputation, so she wrote a note and slipped it to him as she passed his desk. It said, "Earl, I think the principal was mistaken about your being a bad boy. I trust you, and know that you are going to help me make this room the best in the school." Earl not only became a paragon of scholastic virtue but also one of the town's most important people. . . .

It is hard to understand why we are ready to condemn our neighbors and our friends on circumstantial evidence while we are all so determined to see that every criminal has a fair and open trial. Surely we can try to eliminate pride, passion, personal feeling, prejudice, and pettiness from our minds, and show charity to those around us.[16]

So . . . do you occasionally pick out negative characteristics in yourself or others and dwell on them exclusively? You might think you don't. That was my perception until I was forced by my criticism of that administrator to recognize that, in fact, I had misjudged him. When I heard the whisperings of the Spirit tell me I was using selective abstractions in my judgment, I knew I had come to an erroneous conclusion. If I were to accept that truth, I had to become accountable for my behavior. But here is the good part. By becoming accountable, I was able to eliminate the resulting grief that came from my negative judgment. It just disappeared!

Psychologist Carl Rogers said that "the major barrier to mutual interpersonal communication is our very natural tendency to judge."[17] He defends his reasoning with the following illustration: "Now as you leave the meeting tonight, one of the statements that you are likely to hear is, 'I didn't like that man's talk.' Now, what do you respond? Almost invariably your reply will be either approval or disapproval of the attitude expressed. Either you respond, 'I didn't either. I thought that it was terrible,' or else you tend to reply, 'Oh, I thought it was really good.' In other words, regardless of which side you took, your primary reaction is to . . . evaluate [or judge] it from *your* point of view, your own frame of reference."[18]

---

16   "Judge Not, That Ye Be Not Judged," *Ensign*, July 1972, 34.

17   *On Becoming a Person* (New York: Houghton Mifflin, 1995), 330.

18   Ibid., 330–31.

When you express a judgment aloud, your listeners are naturally prompted to make a judgment as well. If they strongly disagree with your judgment, they will probably feel compelled to say so—and, often, the battle lines are drawn. In this way, you immediately subject yourself to the spirit of contention that arises when an individual feels he must defend his views—or his character, as the case may be. In 3 Nephi 11:29, the resurrected Savior taught the Nephites a very important lesson: "For verily, verily I say unto you, he that hath the spirit of contention is not of me, but is of the devil, who is the father of contention, and he stirreth up the hearts of men to contend with anger, one with another."

Again we see that Christ's admonition, "Judge not, that ye be not judged" (Matt. 7:1), spoken of earlier, has reference to both judging others as well as the consequence of doing so. The resulting consequence makes clear the idea that as we sow, so shall we reap (see D&C 6:33). Of course, nothing is easier than finding fault—it requires no talent, no brains, and no character.

Any disagreement we may have with someone results because we unjustly judge that person. It is often the first step toward unnecessary emotional pain. Of course, the more you believe your mind's negative judgments, the more you invite grief into your life. But if you make no unrighteous judgments of others, you will have no grief. Righteous judgment is quite another matter. President Hinckley explains this well:

> I am not asking that all criticism be silenced. Growth comes of correction. Strength comes of repentance. Wise is the man who can acknowledge mistakes pointed out by others and change his course.
>
> What I am suggesting is that each of us turn from the negativism that so permeates our society and look for the remarkable good among those with whom we associate, that we speak of one another's virtues more than we speak of one another's faults.[19]

When we judge others, we provoke God's judgment to be acted upon us, according to the law. The penalty for such negative judgment is often self-inflicted emotional pain. The corollary is also true: the more you refrain from negative judgment, the more peace you will have in your life.

The minute you feel irritated, impatient, scared, sad, angry, or betrayed because of something someone else has said or done (or even something

---

19   Gordon B. Hinckley, "The Continuing Pursuit of Truth," *Ensign*, April 1986, 3–4.

you've said or done), realize that you may be sitting in unrighteous judgment. In such a frame of mind, you will probably focus on that person's incompetence, stupidity, or meanness. Then those thoughts will be repeated over and over in your mind until you virtually have them memorized. At that point, these judgments may bear little resemblance to the truth because your negative perceptions will have been magnified many times over. That warped view becomes your reality because your feelings now reinforce your critical thoughts. Your emotions confirm that you are right and others are wrong, for the "natural man" within us hates to be wrong.

Grief-provoking judgment is not caused solely from judging others but also from harboring envy. For example, when I designed our new home, I had the builder construct a spiral staircase to the roof of the patio. From there I could gaze at the night sky with its majesty of stars and "worlds without end."[20] Of course, from that vantage point during the day, I could also see the expensive cars going down the street and say to myself, *If I had a car like that I would be happy.* I could also see other houses, the majority of them bigger and more expensively built than mine, and say to myself, *If I owned a house as big and as grand as one of those houses, I would be happy.* Such thoughts left me dissatisfied with the wonderful house I already had, creating the illusion that my lot in life was not fair. But if I were to let go of that desire to acquire more, to be admired more, to control more, and so on, then I would be able to see clearly, not being blinded by the bright lights of the tinseled things of this world. Only then would I be protected from the anger and jealousy that would otherwise consume me—all because I might judge myself to be in need of more than I already had. "For where envying . . . is, there is confusion and every evil work" (James 3:16).

One tragic result of passing judgment is that we tend to share those negative judgments with others. When someone makes a mistake, we often make note so we can tell others about it. Commonly known as gossiping, this practice gives us a false sense of superiority because, after finding fault with that person, we consistently think that *we* would never do something as "dumb."

The man or woman who lives with a need to judge others often does so to prove that he or she is always right and better than everyone else. This "need" to be right forces individuals to fight against their own accountability by blaming others. Of course, we really ought to be lenient in our judgment because often the mistakes of others would have been ours had life given

---

20   D&C 76:112.

us the opportunity to make them. Sometimes it is not the pain of life that disturbs us but our judgment of what has caused the pain. You can wipe out that particular pain right now by simply wiping out your negative judgment.

When someone's behavior is tied to our personal feelings, we tend to judge more harshly. This naturally takes place because we have traveled from the impersonal to the personal realm as the relationship becomes more and more intimate. The more devoted one is to someone, the sharper the judgment can be. Perhaps it is this truth that gave rise to the song "You Always Hurt the One You Love."

If we wish to protect ourselves and our loved ones, there can be zero criticism in our personal and intimate relationships. We should accept our loved ones just as they are, with no thought to change them. Of course, if we do not judge them, we will have no desire to criticize them because judgment is a precursor to criticism. Hence, we can again see the wisdom of the simple scripture: "Judge not, that ye be not judged."

FORGIVING OTHERS

Escaping the brambles of unrighteous judgment and its accompanying emotional wounds involves the divine principle of forgiveness, whether we seek to obtain forgiveness for ourselves or to bestow it on someone else.

In D&C 64:10, we read, "I, the Lord, will forgive whom I will forgive, but of you it is required to forgive all men." Or, in the words of Alexander Pope, the famous eighteenth-century poet, "To err is human; to forgive, divine."[21] Without the divine application of forgiveness, judging will continue, potentially creating a major source of anguish and grief. Remember how my judgment of Carolyn's doctors kept me in a continual state of grief. I should have easily forgiven them since they were doing all they could to save her life. I should have focused on how many other lives they had saved. But I was slow to learn. I needed to appeal to the Lord for forgiveness of my sin—my failure to forgive others.

When we muster the courage to forgive others, any accompanying grief that once was associated with that past event is done away with. It disappears. The scriptures testify of this miracle: "Behold, he who has repented of his sins [remember, not to forgive is a sin], the same is forgiven, and I, the Lord, remember them no more" (D&C 58:42). And in Isaiah 1:18, the Lord decreed, "Though your sins be as scarlet, they shall be as white as snow; though they be red like crimson, they shall be as wool."

---

21 Adapted from Pope, "An Essay on Criticism" (London, 1711), 30.

But forgiveness is sometimes difficult because we tend to think in terms of our ofttimes faulty perceptions of right and wrong. Since we do not know why one person thought something to be right, when we so readily "see" its wrongness, we are left with only one opinion: *That person did wrong.* If that is our perception, that is also what we believe. But look at it carefully. In many cases, our lack of forgiveness is the result of our judgment, and our judgment is the result of our own perceptions, which, as we have discovered, are often not all that accurate.

The truth is that we cannot know or understand why someone does something unless we are that person. Only the Lord knows our motives. As Ammon told King Lamoni, the Lord "looketh down upon all the children of men; and he knows all the thoughts and intents of the heart; for by his hand were they all created from the beginning" (Alma 18:32). In many cases, all that is necessary to forgive is to gain understanding. Only truth, not the perception of it, allows understanding, and only understanding opens the door to true forgiveness. But it is often the case, as mentioned above, that we may never understand the motives behind someone's actions because we don't walk in their shoes, so to speak. This is when it becomes especially important to trust that the Lord's commandment to forgive is in our best interest.

But when we *are* blessed to perceive the true motives of others (or to feel how much the Lord loves them), our point of reference is changed. We immediately see them differently. We are able to view their inadequacies with an understanding as to the "why" of their actions. Then we will truly comprehend what Christ said on the cross: "Father, forgive them; for they know not what they do" (Luke 23:34). Even during His Crucifixion, the Savior mercifully acted as the Advocate of those who were responsible for His suffering and death. He only asked His Father, the Almighty Being whose task it is to judge, to forgive them because, as He said, "they know not what they do." His understanding created His forgiveness. In like manner, if we understand the "why" of others' behavior, we will find that there is no need to struggle to forgive what we understand. It occurs naturally.

I know someone who worked hard at keeping in mind all the terrible things someone else had done to him. His mental file kept his grief aflame. Don't keep a mental file (or worse still, a written file) of the details of the ill treatment you have received. Destroy that file. Get it out of your sight and mind. Put an expiration date on all the things your mother, father, husband, wife, or boss (or anyone else) did that caused you grief and throw it away. Repentance is the path to forgiveness and understanding. Follow this path and you will find peace.

Unfortunately, we sometimes "willfully rebel against God" (3 Ne. 6:18). The great poet William Wordsworth once reflected, "And much it griev'd me my heart to think what man has made of man."[22]

We often find it much easier to forgive someone who unknowingly hurt us than it is to forgive someone who purposely did so because we cannot understand why anyone would want to intentionally hurt us. That is what makes it "unforgivable." The actual hurt is the same. The difference is in the mind. The key to unlocking that door of forgiveness, however, is pure and simple. As Christ commanded in the Sermon on the Mount, "Therefore all things whatsoever ye would that men should do to you, do ye even so to them" (Matt. 7:12). This counsel makes clear our responsibility.

It's true that many of our tormentors may never seek our forgiveness, much less the Lord's forgiveness. But holding on to anger only hurts you, not them. Speaking on the subject of forgiving others, President Monson quoted George Herbert, a seventeenth-century poet, who wrote: "He that cannot forgive others breaks the bridge over which he himself must pass if he would ever reach heaven; for everyone has need to be forgiven."[23]

Cooling Someone Else's "Hot" Judgment

I recall a time when I drove my son to the airport. As I pulled up to the curb to let him out, another driver pulled up so close to the back of my car that it was difficult to open the trunk to retrieve my son's luggage. I asked the man if he could back up his car a bit so we could have better access to the trunk. He began shouting obscenities, saying I had cut him off in traffic. He was burning mad, judging me most severely. But instead of apologizing, or at the very least talking kindly to the man, I ignored his verbal abuse, which only put more fuel on his "fire." That was my first mistake. Regardless, I somehow retrieved my son's luggage, hugged him good-bye, and got back into my car to leave.

With a car directly in front of me, I first had to back up to gain enough space to pull out into traffic. The other man had parked so close to me, however, that I inadvertently nudged his bumper with my car. It was not intentional,

---

22   William Wordsworth, Samuel Taylor Coleridge, "Lines Written in Early Spring," *Lyrical Ballads* (Middlesex: The Echo Library, 2007), 54, Google e-book.

23   "The Peril of Hidden Wedges," *Ensign*, July 2007, 6.

nor was it anything that anyone would have paid any attention to under normal circumstances. However, these were not normal circumstances. The man jumped out of his car, came over to my car and, in a rage, kicked it as if it were the offender. I shook my head in disbelief and, with strained self-control, slowly and carefully pulled into traffic, again choosing not to try to reason with him. That was my second mistake. Later, I found he had done serious damage to my car. His kick had produced a dent that cost me hundreds of dollars to repair.

Not long after that bizarre event, I went shopping. As I pulled into a parking stall, I noticed that someone in an approaching car seemed perturbed. Had I taken his parking space? Remembering the airport experience, I jumped out of my car and went to the driver of the other car. "Did I take your parking space?" I inquired. He acknowledged that I had. I quickly apologized, indicating that I was in no hurry and that I would immediately back out to allow him to pull his car into the coveted space. He replied that it was not necessary—that, in fact, I had been there first. With a smile on his face and a wave of his hand, he was off looking for another parking space.

Had I done something similar at the airport, I firmly believe I could have defused the wrath of that man and come to an understanding. I might have easily resolved his anger with just an apologetic word or two, thus brightening his day—and avoiding major damage to my car. The book of Proverbs says it well: "A soft answer turneth away wrath: but grievous words stir up anger" (15:1). As I learned the hard way, sometimes refusing to say anything at all in a wrathful situation can be just as bad as spouting forth "grievous words." The lesson I learned from the airport experience has since served me well. I now recognize that for every minute I spend in any degree of negative judgment or anger, I gain ten times as much grief. Not a good return on my thought investment, is it?

Notably, when asked to sum up his life's guiding principle in a sentence or two, Gandhi simply replied, "Renounce and enjoy."[24] While his statement indicates a more all-inclusive sacrifice than the Lord requires of us today—to renounce all material wealth and possessions to enjoy freedom from worldly cares—our responsibility is to simply renounce all ego-based judgments and enjoy the peace that comes with it.

This same concept is well illustrated in the writings of Chuang Tsze,

---

24   Quoted in Eknath Easwaran, *The Bhagavad Gita* (Tomales, CA: Blue Mountain Center for Meditation, 2007), 1.

a Taoist philosopher. Tsze tells the story of an old man being tossed about in the turbulent waters at the Gorge of Lü. A man standing nearby had seen the man fall into the water. He called his disciples, and together they ran to save the victim. By the time they reached the water, the old man had climbed out onto the bank and was walking along, singing to himself. When asked how he had survived such a watery grave, the old man simply said that he had learned when very young to go down with the water and come up with the water. He said, "I survive because I don't struggle against the water's superior power. That's all."

Like the old man surviving the dangerous turbulent waters, if we release ourselves from making unrighteous judgments, our struggles against the natural man simply disappear. And if we turn our will over to God, we can be guided along by the divine flow of the universe and God's plan for us. As President Ezra Taft Benson firmly testified, "Men and women who turn their lives over to God will discover that He can make a lot more out of their lives than they can. He will deepen their joys, expand their vision, quicken their minds, strengthen their muscles, lift their spirits, multiply their blessings, increase their opportunities, comfort their souls, raise up friends, and pour out peace."[25]

As we yield our agency to the Lord, we will experience an incredible freedom from the cares of the world. Well should we recall this verse in John 14:27: "Peace I leave with you, my peace I give unto you: not as the world giveth, give I unto you. Let not your heart be troubled, neither let it be afraid." Within this state of divine peace, self-deception disappears as new rays of personal accountability and mercy shine forth. And finally, within this state, our increased peace and happiness are continually manifested as we ignore negative judgments and refuse to make negative judgments of our own, for "man shall not smite, neither shall he judge; for judgment is mine, saith the Lord, and vengeance is mine also, and I will repay" (Morm. 8:20). Don't make more work (and grief) for yourself by setting yourself up as a critical judge of others or by judging yourself too harshly.

---

25 "Jesus Christ—Gifts and Expectations," *Ensign*, December 1988, 2.

Chapter Seven

UNMET EXPECTATIONS

IN THE GAME OF GOLF, an ongoing tally is kept of leading players and the number of strokes they make on a big scoreboard (a leaderboard) at the clubhouse. In this manuscript, we have a different kind of leaderboard. It doesn't tell us who is ahead, but in descending order, it does inform us of the kinds of mistakes we can unknowingly make that can cause us grief. For those in my case studies, unmet expectations came in high on their "leaderboard."

They are not alone in ranking unmet expectations high on their list of potential problems. President Kimball once quoted an early (and as-yet unidentified) General Authority of the Church who wrote, "If we are not careful, we can be injured by the frostbite of frustration; we can be frozen in place by the chill of unmet expectations. To avoid this we must—just as we would with arctic coldness—keep moving, keep serving, and keep reaching out, so that our own immobility does not become our chief danger."[26]

His message is clear. If we allow our unrealized expectations to chill our hearts and minds, we will be frozen in our grief, unable to find happiness in what we have right now.

As I studied this particular danger, I could easily relate this concern to many of the events that produced grief in my own life and in the lives of some of my friends. One of these events took place some years ago when I worked as the executive director of a consortium of colleges. Our task was to develop validated instructional programs that could be inexpensively replicated in other colleges throughout the United States, thus improving education on a larger scale.

One evening, after a delightful dinner with the chairman of the board of directors, he told me how hard he had worked through the years with the hope of one day being able to retire and then travel the world over

---

26 "Small Acts of Service," *Ensign*, December 1974, 2.

with his wife and family. He said he now had the financial resources to do so, but an ailing heart would not allow him to take the vacations he had planned. His unmet expectations were manifested when his poor health robbed him of his dream. His narrative cast a pall over the rest of the evening and, unfortunately, over his future life.

In spite of his superior intellect, he lacked understanding of the true source of his grief. In his opinion, the joys of life were over and done. He had given up hope for any great tomorrow and, by so doing, could find no happiness in today. His perceptions caused him to believe that without the capacity to explore the world—something he had planned for and fully expected to be able to do—his life was over. In his mind, all he had left was to wait to die. How sad for him, his wife, and, indeed, his whole family. And all it took was the power of the mind and, very likely the whisperings of the adversary, to sell him that "bill of goods."

My friend actually lived for many more years but not happily, for he was facing the wrong way—inward. His previous abundant life was replaced by one of constant complaint. If only my friend could have embraced the following inspired teachings of President Kimball, when the prophet said:

> The abundant life noted in the scriptures is the spiritual sum that is arrived at by the multiplying of our service to others and by investing our talents in service to God and to man. Jesus said, you will recall, that on the first two commandments hang all the law and the prophets, and those two commandments involve developing our love of God, of self, of our neighbors, and of all men. There can be no real abundance in life that is not connected with the keeping and the carrying out of those two great commandments.[27]

While going through Carolyn's files after she passed away, I found one of her favorite stories, penned by an anonymous hand, that she had often used in her speeches at the Missionary Training Center in Provo, where we happily served for three years. It speaks of the grief that comes when specific expectations are not forthcoming and how that all can change. It is as follows:

> A very poor man, his wife, and two children lived in a small adobe house in a faraway country. There was no indoor

---

27   "The Abundant Life," *Ensign*, July 1978.

plumbing and the beds were simple mats that were rolled out each night on the dirt floor. In spite of their poverty, they were able to live a relatively happy life. That is, until the wife's father passed away, leaving her mother alone without anyone to care for her. According to local custom, that responsibility fell to the next of kin. Two weeks later, the mother moved in with them.

Needless to say, the already crowded conditions of the home were immediately stretched to the breaking point. In desperation, the man trudged forth to seek wisdom from the sage, who lived an uncomplicated life in a cave at the top of the mountain. The man arrived at the entrance to the cave and was granted an audience. After listening quietly to the man's tale of woe, the sage asked him if he had any chickens. He responded that he had three. The sage then told him to move them into the house with the rest of the family and come back and see him in a week's time. Because of the renowned fame of this spiritual teacher, the man, with full faith and trust, returned home and moved the chickens into the house.

Returning home from his work in the fields the following day, the man found his wife in tears. The chickens had caused havoc. While being chased off the single rickety table that occupied the center of the room, they flew into the wooden crate that held the family's only dishes. The crate, hanging precariously on the adobe wall, was knocked to the floor and the dishes were broken. The rest of the week produced much of the same, leaving the wife and her mother in tears.

At the end of the week, the man made his trek to the top of the mountain. He told the sage that having the chickens in the house made life unbearable. He described in some detail how the chickens, and the daily mess they made, had provoked unhappiness for all. With his wretched account of the situation, he thought that the wise centenarian would surely have him move the chickens out of the house. Instead, the old man quietly asked if he had a goat. When the man responded in the affirmative, he leaned over to him and softly whispered, "Move the goat into the house."

Dejectedly, the man returned home and told his wife they were now to move the goat in with them. "How can that be?" the wife exclaimed. "How can we live with a goat and three chickens in our tiny home?" The man made no response but the next day obediently moved the goat into the house.

As you might imagine, the next week was unbelievably bad. Like the chickens, the goat was not housebroken, and the natural results occurred. By the end of the week, the family was in deep despair.

Again the man made the arduous trek to the top of the mountain where the sage listened quietly to his tearful report. After a few minutes of silence and deep meditation, he said to the man, "Move the chickens out of the house and come back and see me in seven days." The man gleefully left, thinking how pleased his wife would be to be rid of the chickens. The next week was better than the previous. While the goat was still there, they had learned to keep a bucket nearby for easier cleanup.

Again the man made the laborious trek to the top of the mountain. This time, the sage listened quietly to the man's upbeat account of a week without the chickens in his home. After a few minutes of silence, the sage advised, "Move the goat out of the house and come back and see me in seven day's time." The man practically danced down the mountain. Can you imagine the joy that he and his wife experienced as they moved the goat out of the house, allowing the animal to relieve herself at will and eat the green grass of her choosing? In spite of the strong barnyard smell that still permeated the house, life was greatly improved.

At the end of the week, the man again made his regular visit to the Seer. This time the journey was not even tiring. His feet fairly flew up the mountain. He could hardly wait to tell of his improved life. The sage listened quietly to the man's enthusiastic account. After a few minutes of silence, the sage asked the man, "Are you now happy?" The man could not contain his pleasure as he again reiterated his newfound joy. "Go, then," admonished the sage, "and live in peace with your wife, your mother-in-law, and your children."

When you find yourself discontented because what you expected did not come to pass, you may grow unhappy, probably not because of any external conditions, but because of your own preconceived ideas of what you *think* you need in order to be happy. Truly, it's not what you think you need that will make you happy; it's in knowing that you already have what you need. When you dispel those preconceived "needs," like the humble man in the story, you will find liberation from your self-imposed grief.

A friend told me a story of a young mother who was disconsolate over giving birth to a baby girl instead of the boy she had so desperately wanted. When feeding time came, a wise nurse went to the nursery, took a baby boy who had a small facial deformity, and quietly slipped him into the arms of the melancholy mother. The mother exclaimed, "This is not my baby!" The nurse's response was, "Well, this is an infant boy. Maybe its mother will be willing to trade babies with you." At that moment, the young mother had a change of heart. She no longer desired something more than what she had but was instantly happy with the special blessing of having a *healthy* baby girl. She immediately loved the child she had and saw no need for anything more.

Sometimes we feel discouraged when our expectations are thwarted because of the greed, cruelty, or deceptions of those around us. We often bow under the heaviness of misfortunes others have created for us. Our thoughts protest, saying, *This is wrong. It's not fair. It is cruel and unjust. Why did this happen to me?* And in the agony and intensity of these feelings, we half unconsciously repeat these thoughts in monotonous iterations as if somehow that repetition will magically bring relief. Tracking these noisy thoughts will not bring us peace, as I can personally attest. It will bring us renewed grief if we do not learn to let go.

President Kimball had this to say about such injustice. He explained, "This life, this narrow sphere we call mortality, does not, within the short space of time we are allowed here, give to all of us perfect justice, perfect health, or perfect opportunities. Perfect justice, however, will come eventually through a divine plan, as will the perfection of all other conditions and blessings—to those who have lived to merit them."[28]

---

28 "The Abundant Life" 2.

The only way to avoid such suffering at the hands of others would be to deny agency to all, and that, of course, was Satan's corrupt plan: "Wherefore, because that Satan rebelled against me, and sought to destroy the agency of man, which I, the Lord God, had given him, . . . I caused that he should be cast down" (Moses 4:3).

To answer the question of "Why?" in another way, the Lord has revealed that such trials happen to you, as they happen to us all, because "it must needs be, that there is an opposition in all things" (2 Ne. 2:11). Without them we could not progress. As Brigham Young once taught, "You cannot give any persons their exaltation unless they know what evil is, what sin, sorrow, and misery are, for no person could comprehend, appreciate, and enjoy an exaltation upon any other principle."[29]

We learn from sad experience that when people treat you poorly, they do so because they have listened to the natural man. Of course, the Christlike course of action is to learn how to respond to those who are listening to the natural man's ill-conceived advice so we do not cause them additional grief. We must recognize that this entire process first takes place in the mind. Think for a moment. You shouldn't be angry with a cannibal if he wants to eat you for dinner. It's what cannibals do. To them, it's not unjust—it's simply their way of survival. It is also silly to become angry with a truck driver who is slow in passing another truck because of his heavy load, thus blocking your lane of traffic. That's how it is as they move their goods to market. You can choose to patiently ignore the inconvenience— and the grief that otherwise would have been yours. Ignore the things that you can do nothing about and remain happy. Or, try seeing them in a different light. In speaking of this, Elder Joseph B. Wirthlin wrote:

> The first thing we can do is learn to laugh. Have you ever seen an angry driver who, when someone else makes a mistake, reacts as though that person has insulted his honor, his family, his dog, and his ancestors all the way back to Adam? Or have you had an encounter with an overhanging cupboard door left open at the wrong place and the wrong time which has been cursed, condemned, and avenged by a sore-headed victim?
>
> There is an antidote for times such as these: learn to laugh.
>
> I remember loading up our children in a station wagon and driving to Los Angeles. There were at least nine of us in

the car, and we would invariably get lost. Instead of getting angry, we laughed. Every time we made a wrong turn, we laughed harder.

Getting lost was not an unusual occurrence for us. Once while heading south to Cedar City, Utah, we took a wrong turn and didn't realize it until two hours later when we saw the "Welcome to Nevada" signs. We didn't get angry. We laughed, and as a result, anger and resentment rarely resulted. Our laughter created cherished memories for us.

I remember when one of our daughters went on a blind date. She was all dressed up and waiting for her date to arrive when the doorbell rang. In walked a man who seemed a little old, but she tried to be polite. She introduced him to me and my wife and the other children; then she put on her coat and went out the door. We watched as she got into the car, but the car didn't move. Eventually our daughter got out of the car and, red faced, ran back into the house. The man that she thought was her blind date had actually come to pick up another of our daughters who had agreed to be a babysitter for him and his wife.

We all had a good laugh over that. In fact, we couldn't stop laughing. Later, when our daughter's real blind date showed up, I couldn't come out to meet him because I was still in the kitchen laughing. Now, I realize that our daughter could have felt humiliated and embarrassed. But she laughed with us, and as a result, we still laugh about it today.

The next time you're tempted to groan, you might try to laugh instead. It will extend your life and make the lives of all those around you more enjoyable.[30]

Truly, humor can be an antidote to suffering. It all really does hinge on how we look at things. President John Taylor once observed, "We have learned many things through suffering. We call it suffering. I call it a school of experience. I never did bother my head much about these things. I do not today. What are these things for? Why is it that good men should be tried? . . . I have never looked at these things in any other light than trials for the purpose of purifying the Saints of God that they

---

30　"Come What May, and Love It," *Ensign,* November 2008.

may be, as the scriptures say, as gold that has been seven times purified by the fire."[31] How would we ever be tried if everything went as expected? We grow only when we learn to accept what life brings and to love life in spite of its difficulties. Otherwise, we remain spiritual infants, never realizing our capacity as sons and daughters of God who have been tried and proven in the furnace of affliction. Otherwise, we remain little better than the laboratory rats described in the story that follows.

Dr. Beall once told me of a study that affirms this notion of unmet expectations. He explained that to test this concept with laboratory rats, the behavioral scientists created a special environment for them, giving them everything a rat could want. Then, one by one, all of the amenities were taken away until their environment was like that of any other rats. The scientists discovered that once this occurred, the rats' behavior radically changed—some even became violent. They had been previously trained to expect certain pleasures, and when those pleasures were taken away, the rats could not mask their reaction to their unmet expectations. The scientists deduced that if these rats had never experienced fancier accommodations, they wouldn't have acted out in displeasure.

Could it be that our society has created such excessive expectations that when they are not met, we have reactions like the laboratory rats? Does a newly engaged couple justify putting themselves into debt to buy expensive wedding rings just because our society equates gold and big diamonds with love? Does our culture glorify violence so much that bullied teens feel they have every right to turn a gun on their classmates? Does the media place so much pressure on women and girls to be unrealistically slender that they will do anything, including becoming bulimic, so as to achieve those worldly expectations? Is this what happens when rude drivers feel entitled to certain road rights and privileges to the extent that the rights and privileges of others do not count? Don't allow this kind of attitude to take up residence inside your mind. It can only end in grief.

As a pilot, my son Steven told me that the number-one cause of crashes in private planes is pilot error. The same is true in life. Whenever we "crash and burn," the number-one reason is human error. Somewhere along the road, we did something that could have been avoided. The sadness is that we often actually know better. We just chose to experiment a little: *I think I'll have a beer with my friends. After all, what is one little beer going to hurt?* Or, *I think I'll have a smoke. After all, what is one little cigarette going to*

---

31 *Deseret News*, Semi-Weekly, October 28, 1884, 1.

matter? Then when that one drink eventually leads to alcoholism or that one cigarette eventually leads to nicotine addiction—or to illegal drug use—we are unhappy. After all, that is not what we expected.

While we may have regrets over past expectations, we need not think that they should forever shroud us in grief. Pain and guilt from past mistakes and unmet expectations are part of the learning process. We cannot change our past mistakes and unmet expectations, but we can learn to accept them for what they are—foundations for making wise decisions in the future. That is their inherent value—if we humble ourselves and apply the Atonement in our lives. As the Savior instructed, "For behold, I, God, have suffered these things for all, that they might not suffer if they would repent; But if they would not repent they must suffer even as I; Which suffering caused myself, even God, the greatest of all, to tremble because of pain, and to bleed at every pore, and to suffer both body and spirit—and would that I might not drink the bitter cup, and shrink" (D&C 19:16–18).

Unless we confess, forsake, and repent of our sins, we will have gained nothing but pain and condemnation. What good does it do if we reject the Atonement and insist on holding on to our grief? "What doth it profit a man if a gift is bestowed upon him, and he receive not the gift? Behold, he rejoices not in that which is given unto him, neither rejoices in him who is the giver of the gift" (D&C 88:33).

Learning these lessons in this school of life is not for the faint of heart. It can be tough. Ask the infirm who struggle just to get out of bed—or those who can't even do that. Some of the most steadfast prophets and disciples, including Lehi, the Apostle Paul, and the Prophet Joseph Smith, have felt overwhelmed at times with the grievous trials of life. But once we understand life's purpose, as they did, and learn to rely on the Lord for succor, life can be more than just manageable—it can be glorious! When life's learning process becomes clear to the mind and the heart, we can shift more easily toward a more congenial relationship between where we are and where we would like to be. Based on this understanding, we can adjust our expectations to focus on the goals that matter most. Then, if things go awry, we won't get lost in our grief because our unmet expectations will just be one more integral piece in the learning process of our lives.

Ironically, we often learn more from our trials than from the outright blessings we receive. To offer a personal example, I am a cancer survivor, and in my fight against that disease I greatly increased my capacity to understand how to find peace and contentment despite my suffering. It is often from these hard experiences that we discover who we are and derive the meaning of life. This process of growth is cumulative, with each experience building upon another as we ascend in wisdom from one capacity to another. True, we sometimes have setbacks, but even then we can reach new heights. And as we progress step by step, it is good to remember that it doesn't matter if we are near the top of the stairs or near the bottom. What matters is the direction in which we are heading.

Life's lessons are not unlike a competitive game of football. We all flock to see our favorite team play. Even when someone fumbles the ball, we keep cheering them on. Similarly, in life we may not like a particular play, but we must remember that it is just one play out of many. We must keep going, even when we are the ones who fumble the ball, because we know the game is not over. Even if we suffer setbacks in life (lose ten yards), we cannot allow our thwarted attempts to score a touchdown stop us from trying again on the next down. After all, the game of life is not a test of speed but of endurance—even if all we can manage is advancing just a few yards at a time. As the Lord declared in D&C 14:7, "If you keep my commandments and endure to the end you shall have eternal life, which gift is the greatest of all the gifts of God." That is the touchdown we want to score. Don't let unmet expectations get in the way of achieving it.

Chapter Eight
MISPLACED BLAME AND DECEPTION

I WAS SURPRISED AT THE diverse categories identified by the people in my studies as being responsible for someone's grief. Misplaced blame and deception were linked together because they were seen as one package by those who experienced the pain they caused. In addition, when the tallies were counted, self-deception and misplaced blame were tied, both ranking equally high on the list of things that caused grief.

Frankly, until I found out how much grief these two items caused, I had not even thought of their danger. I should have been more aware of it because the scriptures often point out the importance of seeking the truth, something those who blame and deceive do not do. To falsely blame and self-deceive is to lie. In Jacob we read: "The Spirit speaketh the truth and lieth not. Wherefore, it speaketh of things as they really are, and of things as they really will be; wherefore, these things are manifested unto us plainly, for the salvation of our souls" (Jacob 4:13; see also D&C 93:24).

When we speak of things as they really are, we have arrived at Kubler-Ross's final stage of grief: acceptance. When we finally accept things as they really are, we accept the truth. It is, as always, the truth that sets us free (see John 8:32). But those who would falsely blame and deceive are not true to themselves or others. In the final analysis, they will eventually reap grief as their reward for being false.

Being true is the path to happiness. Being false is the path to grief. Those who would deceive not only their neighbor but also themselves are prime candidates for eventual sorrow. For instance, in the preface of *Leadership and Self-Deception*, the authors explore the problem of misplaced blame through an analogy of a baby girl learning to crawl. As it happens, she starts pushing herself backward instead of forward. As a result, she often gets lodged beneath the furniture. Of course, the more she tries to get out of her predicament, the more stuck she becomes. As the authors relate, "If this infant could talk, she would blame the furniture for her troubles. After all, she is doing everything that she can think of. The problem couldn't be *hers*. But of course the problem is hers."[32]

When my children were growing up, it was not uncommon to find something amiss and to hear my other sons say, "Bob did it." Sometimes Bob did indeed do it, but often he did not. By shifting the blame, whoever did it failed himself . . . and Bob.

Of course it is natural to silently feel relieved when an unpleasant situation turns out to be someone else's fault. Being thus conditioned, we too may want to place blame on someone or something else the next time a problem arises. But beware. By directly or indirectly blaming someone else for our own indiscretions, we deceive ourselves and by so doing we impede our opportunity to learn the lessons we might have otherwise learned. The faster we learn to accept accountability, the faster we will be able to confront and unburden ourselves of the grief resulting from our actions or thoughts.

Take the case of an inattentive motorist driving on the freeway. Without checking his blind spot or signaling, he starts to merge into the left lane. Another driver who is already in the left-hand lane attempting to pass must quickly apply his brakes so as not to be hit. Just at that moment, our irresponsible driver sees the other car and swerves back into his lane. As the passing motorist cautiously goes around him, our wayward driver shakes his fist at the other, choosing to blame rather than taking accountability for his own failure to be more cautious.

Since learning does not occur until accountability takes place, that motorist will surely continue the same ill-conceived behavior, repeatedly placing himself and others in danger—deceiving himself by blaming others. But in reality, the more blame he tries to unload on others, the more grief he will pile upon himself. Until he learns to be accountable, his life, as well as the lives of others, may be put in emotional, spiritual, or physical jeopardy.

When people fail at something, they should be grateful to know that it was their fault, for then the solution lies in their own hands. Individuals who knowingly blame others for something they did will surely worsen their errors and grief by trying to deceive others as well as themselves. Such people

---

32 The Arbinger Institute, *Leadership and Self-Deception: Getting out of the Box* (San Francisco: Berrett-Koehler Publishers, 2010), xi.

will find that in their predisposition to blame others for their mistakes, they experience a boomerang effect—no matter how much effort they put into "throwing" the blame back on others, their mistakes will, sooner or later, always come right back at them. Like lies, mistakes multiply readily.

The natural man in us works to have us believe that blame exists "out there" instead of within each of us. If people believe all faults exist "out there" (it's the "natural" thing to do), they can neither identify nor resolve the true source of their problems. But the sin, the error, or whatever it is that keeps us from reaching our highest potential—rarely originates completely "out there." Many problems originate from within. But we have been conditioned to blame our environment or others for much of the suffering in our life.

Elder Hugh W. Pinnock said: "We are living in a strange time. It has been called the space age or computer age. However, it seems to be the age of blaming everyone and everything for any unfavorable condition."[33] We blame our boss, our parents, the weather, the economy, our spouse, our enemies, our lack of money—anyone or anything that seems to fit. The one person we don't blame is the person who is generally responsible—ourselves.

But there is an answer: If something doesn't work out like you planned, simply ask yourself, "How did I help create or contribute to that problem?" Retrace your steps until you find where you might have done or said something that would have led to a more positive outcome. (Remember the irate driver who kicked a dent in my car? That was one I might have easily prevented.) Armed with that mindset, you will often see that, indeed, you could have positively influenced the outcome of any number of issues and by so doing eliminated your grief. Just remember the guideline: when faced with a problem, always consider the possibility that you may have helped create it in some way. Make the fault all about *you* (unless and until proven otherwise) and see what solutions may appear.

Self-deception usually begins with a self-centered choice. Take the case of the man who borrows his wife's car but chooses not to refill the gas tank before he returns it. Of course he first has to justify that choice to himself: "It won't hurt her to fill up her own car. I'm too busy, and she has more time than I do. She probably won't even notice." These are just a few of the thoughts that could easily go through his mind. With these thoughts, he soon sees himself as the hardworking victim with a multitude of important things to do—which preclude his putting gas in his wife's

---

33 "Now Is the Time," *Ensign*, May 1989, 10.

car—thus unfairly making her time and responsibilities less important than his own.

Armed with all of these selfish reasons, he justifies his behavior. Once that is accomplished, he is satisfied that his actions are right and that his wife will be wrong if she objects. Certainly his spouse will not feel inclined to agree with him as she hurries to arrive at an appointment only to find that her car is nearly out of gas. When the man and his spouse next meet, his self-serving decision will probably lead to a heated discussion. In his self-deception, he will have created avoidable grief for the both of them. President Kimball once declared, "Almost all dishonesty owes its existence and growth to that inward distortion we call self-justification. It is the first, and worst, and most insidious form of cheating: We are cheating ourselves."[34]

The path to self-deception is clearly marked. It begins when we allow our behavior to be guided by the tendencies of the natural man. In such cases, our self-centered behavior has to be justified, usually in a distorted or roundabout way. Based on these vain justifications, we blame others because they stand in the way of what we want (what the ego says we "need"). Of course, the more we justify our behavior, the more others become at fault. When we succumb to our self-interest, our view merely reflects our own overriding, misguided, and selfish desires. We must ask ourselves this: do we "undertake to cover our sins, or to gratify our pride, our vain ambition" (D&C 121:37)? If so, we are not seeing things as they really are; we are seeing them as *we* really are.

When we learn to recognize our perceptual errors, looking past them as lessons learned, we are humbled, opening the way for us to access the Atonement so as to forgive others and ourselves. Then we will be able to focus on living God-centered truths, becoming the Christlike individuals we were created to become. It is in this manner that we can access governing truths and override dangerous false perceptions.

These truths protect and inspire because they are spirit based—they cannot exist apart from God because all truth resides in God. When appearing in His resurrected form to His doubting apostles, Thomas and Philip, the Savior said, "I am the way, the truth, and the life: no man cometh unto the Father, but by me. If ye had known me, ye should have known my Father also: and from henceforth ye know him, and have seen him" (John 14:6–7). Indeed, He is "a God of truth, and [can]not lie" (Ether 3:12).

---

34 "On My Honor," *Ensign*, April 1979, 2.

One of the authors of *Leadership and Self-Deception* points out an occasion when he deceived himself into thinking his comfort was more important than simple courtesy. He recalls:

> About a year ago, I flew from Dallas to Phoenix on a flight that had open seating. I'd arrived early enough to have a rather early boarding number. While boarding, I overheard the boarding agent say that the plane was not sold out but that there would be very few unoccupied seats. I felt lucky and relieved to find a window seat open with a vacant seat beside it about a third of the way back on the plane. Passengers still in need of seats continued streaming down the aisle, their eyes scanning and evaluating the desirability of their dwindling options. I set my briefcase on the vacant middle seat, took out the day's paper, and started to read. I remember peering over the top corner of the paper at the people who were coming down the aisle. At the sight of body language that said my briefcase's seat was being considered, I spread the paper wider, making the seat look as undesirable as possible.[35]

The interesting thing about self-deception is how fast it gathers strength. First we selfishly choose—then we have to justify our choice so as to be right. That justification, often established on a false premise, leads to additional choices with their added justification. Thus it goes, on and on, until the perpetrator has primed himself for an explosion.

We may think that self-deception is a trivial matter. It is not. If allowed to grow, it can be catastrophic. A good case in point is Timothy McVeigh. After years of self-deception he arrived at the point that he felt compelled to bomb a federal building in Oklahoma, killing 168 men, women, and children. He never exhibited any remorse for the grief he caused the thousands of extended family members and friends of those he killed because he had totally justified his actions in his mind. He was not to blame. It was the government's fault. And so it goes.

Happiness in this life is the direct result of how well we follow our inner "light of Christ" (Moro. 7:18) and "hearken unto the Spirit" (2 Ne. 32:8) so as to overcome any form of self-deception. It is the gift of the Spirit that "will show unto you all things what ye should do" (2 Ne. 32:5).

---

35   The Arbinger Institute, *Leadership and Self-Deception: Getting out of the Box*, 31.

Popular author Wayne Dyer cited an equally popular poem that sums up rather well the direction we all should be taking:

> People are often unreasonable, illogical and self-centered;
> Forgive them anyway.
> If you are kind, people may accuse you of selfish, ulterior motives;
> Be kind anyway.
> If you are successful, you will win some false friends and some true enemies;
> Succeed anyway.
> If you are honest and frank, people may cheat you;
> Be honest and frank anyway.
> What you spend years building, someone may destroy overnight;
> Build anyway.
> If you find serenity and happiness, some may be jealous;
> Be happy anyway.
> The good you do today, people will often forget tomorrow;
> Do good anyway.
> Give the world the best you have, and it may never be enough;
> Give the world the best you've got anyway.
> You see, in the final analysis, it is all between you and God;
> It was never between you and them . . . anyway.[36]

Remember, much of our personal sadness is created when we deceive ourselves regarding who is to blame for our difficulties or in regard to what we think we need to be happy. Much of our joy in life takes place when we come to realize that we are responsible for everything we do, say, or think. It is then that we also realize that we are independent agents, free to act and not to be acted upon. As President Kimball wisely taught, "There are those today who say that man is the result of his environment and cannot rise above it. Those who justify mediocrity, failure, immorality of all kinds, and even weakness and criminality are certainly misguided. Surely the environmental conditions found in childhood and youth are an influence

---

36 "The Final Analysis," in Wayne Dyer, *There Is a Spiritual Solution to Every Problem*, 109–110.

of power. But the fact remains that every normal soul has its free agency and the power to row against the current and to lift itself to new planes of activity and thought and development. Man *can* transform himself. Man *must* transform himself."[37]

Contemplate this anonymous legend of a Cherokee Indian teaching his grandson about life. It goes like this:

> "A fight is going on inside me," he said to the boy. "It is a terrible fight and it is between two wolves. One is evil—he is anger, envy, sorrow, regret, greed, arrogance, self-pity, guilt, resentment, inferiority, lies, false pride, superiority, and ego." He continued. "The other is good—he is joy, peace, love, hope, serenity, humility, kindness, benevolence, empathy, generosity, truth, compassion, and faith.
>
> This same fight is going on inside you, and inside every other person, too."
>
> The grandson thought about it for a minute and then asked his grandfather, "Which wolf will win?"
>
> The old Cherokee simply replied, "The one you feed."[38]

Misplaced blame first originates within the mind. If we listen to those impressions we can be left with the nonstop push and pull of the human experience, guessing and wondering what to do as we face serious, recurring problems in our work, our relationships, our finances, our health, etc. If we want to overcome these problems, we have to become responsible for everything in life that the Lord has placed in our control. This includes the quality of our thoughts, feelings, achievements, and relationships as well as the state of our physical fitness, income, debts—everything! Given that it only takes some dedication, a bit of practice, and an awareness of the importance to not self-deceive, we can become more accountable for our actions. We can overcome our propensity for self-deception.

---

37   "The Abundant Life," *Ensign*, July 1978, 3; emphasis added.

38   As quoted in Patrick Snow, *Creating Your Own Destiny: How to Get Exactly What You Want Out of Life and Work* (Hoboken, NJ: John Wiley & Sons, 2010), 92.

Chapter Nine

FAITH VERSUS FEAR

WHEN ANALYZING THE DATA FROM my research studies, the subject of fear repeatedly surfaced as a contributing factor for grief. Contrary to my surprise at finding misplaced blame and deception high on that same scoreboard, I actually expected fear to be ranked high. I supposed that such would be the case because I had experienced a pretty high level of fear when Carolyn passed away. Mine was not fear of her dying, me dying, or the prospect of passing on to a nothingness. These were not part of my belief system. My issue lay in thinking my future seemed destined to be one of ultimate uncertainty—the simple fear of what to do next, whereas for my wife, it was one of peaceful passage from mortality to immortality. Anxiety filled the void in my lack of personal clarity regarding this separation. And that only compounded my ever-increasing grief.

Of course, I am not the only one to experience these feelings. In his book *A Grief Observed*, C. S. Lewis (who also lost his wife to cancer) wrote, "No one ever told me that grief felt so like fear."[39] He is absolutely right. That is exactly how I felt.

That basic lack of understanding about death presents the universal question: is there life after death? In *The Tibetan Book of the Living and Dying*, the author notes that the master teachers in that religion often ask their members if they believe in a life after this one. He goes on to note, "They are not being asked whether they believe in it as a philosophical proposition, but whether they feel it deeply in their heart. The master knows that if people believe in a life after this one, their whole outlook on their existence will be different, and they will have a distinct sense of personal responsibility and morality."[40] For those with a testimony

---

39 *A Grief Observed* (New York: HarperCollins, 1961), 3.

40 Sogyal Rinpoche, Patrick Gaffney, and Andrew Harvey, *The Tibetan Book of Living and Dying* (San Francisco: HarperSanFrancisco, 2002), 9.

of the gospel of Jesus Christ, death is not to be glamorized, feared, or trivialized but is to be understood as another step in the continuation of life. President Wilford Woodruff wrote at length on this subject:

> Without the gospel of Christ the separation by death is one of the most gloomy subjects that it is possible to contemplate; but just as soon as we obtain the gospel and learn the principle of the resurrection the gloom, sorrow and suffering occasioned by death are, in a great measure, taken away. I have often thought that, to see a dead body, and to see that body laid in the grave and covered with earth, is one of the most gloomy things on earth; without the gospel it is like taking a leap in the dark. But as quick as we obtain the gospel, as soon as the spirit of man is enlightened by the inspiration of the Almighty, he can exclaim with one of old— "Oh grave, where is thy victory, Oh death, where is thy sting? . . . " [See 1 Cor. 15:55–57.] The resurrection of the dead presents itself before the enlightened mind of man, and he has a foundation for his spirit to rest upon.[41]

Fear of death and a disbelief in an afterlife not only increases one's grief, it also creates a greater potential for the destruction of oneself, others, and even the planet. Some of those who think that life ends at death see no reason not to adopt the "drink and be merry, for tomorrow we die" attitude (2 Ne. 28:7). They see nothing wrong with pursuing riotous lifestyles, mistreating others, or even plundering the earth's resources for their own selfish ends.

Many fear death because it is the end of everything they know. To those without faith in an afterlife, death represents the abrupt end to everything, including their association with those they love. I suspect that these people are often emotionally pushed into a dark abyss, that they feel lost and bewildered. For those who do not believe in a life hereafter, death is losing what they have fought so vigilantly to maintain—their bodies, their relationships, their experiences, everything. But a testimony of the plan of salvation shifts our perception of death entirely. As President Woodruff reflected, "When mourning the loss of our departed friends, I cannot help but think that in every death there is a birth; the spirit leaves the body dead to us, and passes to the other side of the veil alive to that

---

41 *Deseret News*, Semi-Weekly, July 20, 1875, 1.

great and noble company that are also working for the accomplishment of the purposes of God, in the redemption and salvation of a fallen world."[42]

We should remember, however, that the only things we can take with us when we die are what we have learned and what we have become (see D&C 130:18). So if we are selfish and egotistical in life, we will continue to be selfish and egotistical when we die. The passing of such a wasted life will be filled with the regret of what might have been. That is the only fear we should have of death—a fear that we will not hear the Savior speak the words, "Well done, good and faithful servant" (Matt. 25:23).

Those who die unprepared for death because of their ill-conceived deeds are the same ones who have lived unprepared for life. To be prepared for one is to be prepared for the other. Don't make your life a celebration of the insignificant. Do something meaningful for yourself and others as often as possible. Build a bridge over to the next life upon the solid pillars of the principles that matter most. Then you will be prepared to cross over into the next life because "if ye are prepared ye shall not fear" (D&C 38:30). But how do we prepare ourselves? Moroni explained it so: "Be wise in the days of your probation; strip yourselves of all uncleanness; ask not, that ye may consume it on your lusts, but ask with a firmness unshaken, that ye will yield to no temptation, but that ye will serve the true and living God" (9:28).

Since the only things that we can take with us to the other side are what we have learned and what we have become, these are the things we should "be about" here. To find meaning in one's life across the veil is to have meaning in one's life on this side of that veil. As we make every moment here an opportunity to prepare for the life beyond, we will overcome our grief and find happiness both here and there. Death is not to be feared but simply to be continually prepared for. It is in this preparation that we can magnify our happiness here—and there. For those who have learned how to live by divine principles and hearken unto the Spirit, death will come not as defeat but as a great victory. Don't wait for a crisis in your life to bring you to an awakening.

In *Man's Search For Meaning* (Victor E. Frankl's book about his imprisonment during World War II in the Auschwitz concentration camp), Frankl wrote that when his fellow prisoners lost their faith in a better future, they were doomed. He tells the story of one of his friends who had a dream.

---

42   *The Discourses of Wilford Woodruff*, sel. G. Homer Durham (Salt Lake City, UT: Bookcraft, 1946), 245.

In the dream a voice told him that he could ask anything he might want to know and that his questions would be answered. The friend asked when he would be liberated and his sufferings would come to an end. Frankl reported that when this occurred, it was the beginning of March, and the voice in the dream told his friend he would be liberated on March thirtieth. As the thirtieth drew nearer, it appeared very unlikely that he would be freed on the promised date, and the friend lost his faith. On March twenty-ninth, he suddenly became delirious and lost consciousness. On March thirty-first, he was dead. His faith in the future and his will to live had become paralyzed, and his body fell victim to illness.[43]

Faith can carry and sustain us even in the face of seemingly insurmountable odds, but in order for faith to banish fear, that faith must be based in a knowledge of the truth. It must be centered in the source of all truth—in the Lord Jesus Christ. In the Bible we read of how knowledge confirms faith and how faith repels fear. Consider that when Christ was faced with a threatening storm, a storm that had His disciples fearing for their lives, He simply commanded the elements to be still: "And, behold, there arose a great tempest in the sea, insomuch that the ship was covered with the waves: but he was asleep. And his disciples came to him, and awoke him, saying, Lord, save us: we perish. And he saith unto them, Why are ye fearful, O ye of little faith? Then he arose, and rebuked the winds and the sea; and there was a great calm" (Matt. 8:24–26).

The message that is sometimes missed in this short scripture relates to His first question: "Why are ye fearful?" Because of their fear, they had limited their faith. To increase your faith, you must decrease your fear, for fear is the opposite of faith. By so doing you will automatically increase your spiritual understanding. "For God hath not given us the spirit of fear; but of power, and of love, and of a sound mind" (2 Tim. 1:7).

Remember when Christ walked on the water as recorded in Matthew 14:25–31? This poignant passage reads:

> And in the fourth watch of the night Jesus went unto them, walking on the sea.
>
> And when the disciples saw him walking on the sea, they were troubled, saying, It is a spirit; and they cried out for fear.
>
> But straightway Jesus spake unto them, saying, Be of good cheer; it is I; be not afraid.

---

43   Victor E. Frankl, *Man's Search for Meaning* (New York: Simon & Schuster, 1984). 95–96.

And Peter answered him and said, Lord, if it be thou, bid me come unto thee on the water.

And he said, Come. And when Peter was come down out of the ship, he walked on the water, to go to Jesus.

But when he saw the wind boisterous, he was afraid; and beginning to sink, he cried, saying, Lord, save me.

And immediately Jesus stretched forth his hand, and caught him, and said unto him, O thou of little faith, wherefore didst thou doubt?

I suspect that in our own grief too many of us turn our thoughts to the fear of "what might be," not to "what is" as we too see the "boisterous winds" of life. One cannot actively deal with something that might be but only with what is.

I remember that some years ago I took my father across the border into Calexico, Mexico. I parked the car, and we took a stroll down a little street looking for a good place to eat. While standing on a street corner waiting for the light to change, my father became agitated as he listened to a group of young people nearby. "Why is that gang of hooligans talking about us?" he whispered to me. Unfamiliar with the language as well as his surroundings, his fear had him worrying that the animated youth were members of a dangerous street gang. Because I speak Spanish, I knew they had just left a soccer match and were still talking about the game.

I turned to them and asked if they could recommend a good place to eat. They could not have been more helpful and engaging, offering to accompany us to a restaurant known for its good food. As we all walked together, I teased them, saying that their favorite team consisted of a bunch of losers. They teased me right back, saying that as a gringo my understanding of the game of *fútbol* was sorely lacking. When we reached the restaurant, my father shook hands with each of them, thanking them in English for their kindness. They may not have understood his words, but they understood his engaging smile.

On that occasion, my father saw an unfamiliar environment and its inhabitants as hazardous; this generated a fear of what he thought was a potential danger. Of course he listened to his fear. Why would he not? Terrorists use it. Gangs use it. The schoolyard bully uses it. The abusive husband or wife uses it. Even the world seems much more obsessed with fear than with hope. Just look at its proliferation in the media, which seems far more likely to chronicle the day's horrible events than anything positive.

Fear sells! It was only when my father was armed with the knowledge of the truth that he was able to put his fear aside. He then had faith in those young men because he knew their intentions were honorable.

It is our fear of the unknown (our lack of knowledge) that keeps getting in the way. Clearly, faith and knowledge are prerequisites to overcoming fear because, as previously noted, faith and knowledge keep close company. In the inspiring hymn, "How Firm a Foundation," we are told, "Fear not, I am with thee; oh, be not dismayed. For I am thy God and will still give thee aid. I'll strengthen thee, help thee, and cause thee to stand, Upheld by my righteous, . . . omnipotent hand" (*Hymns*, no. 85).

There is no limit to what grief our fearful thoughts may generate. They tell us we may lose our jobs, our sweetheart, our health, our everything. These thoughts can cause paranoia, stress, obsession, jealousy, and even neurotic disorders and depression. Doubt and fear limit the scope of our vision and our physical and spiritual growth. Fear of not being good enough, big enough, thin enough, humble enough, proud enough, smart enough, or rich enough creates nothing but trouble. Some of our anxious thoughts are legitimate, but when carefully examined, most are overblown or imaginary, planted there by the adversary—and they lead us only to grief.

Since most fear is unfounded, so is its accompanying grief. Fear is primarily a mental reaction to what *might* happen, not to what is actually taking place. And if you dwell on your fear long enough, your thoughts can become toxic and harmful. For example, if your fear causes you to perceive yourself as unworthy and unloved, then that is what you will project to others, and you will not have the faith to see yourself otherwise. Contrarily, if you see yourself as God sees you, with love for and hope in yourself and others, you will project that, thinking and acting accordingly. Your self-confidence will expand, as will your faith! Your tightly held outside view registers how much joy you will allow yourself to see and experience.

You can only give of what you have. If you have resentment, that is what you will give. If you have false pride, that too is what you will give. If you judge and criticize others or often feel offended and put upon by others, then these are the things you can contribute—a poor contribution indeed. But if you are kind and considerate, if you love yourself and others, if you have hope for the future, if you are selfless with your time and talents, and if you offer words of appreciation to God and those around you, then these are the spiritual gifts you will give to the world. As the Lord commands,

"Let your light so shine before men, that they may see your good works, and glorify your Father which is in heaven" (Matt. 5:16).

One who daily lives in fear is simply watching the projection of a horror movie on the "stage" of his mind. Such a person calls forth the actors, asking each one in turn to play out the scene of his impending danger, unfairness, or scarcity. Such people may even revel in their tribulations, seeking pity from those who may listen to their sad tale of woe, thus further closing their eyes to the liberties and blessings that could be theirs. They allow their fears to overcome their faith—to conceal and obscure their potential as divine children of God. Unfortunately, those motivated by fear will continue in this path until they discover that there is no happiness to be found in fear—that happiness can only be found through our good works and expressed through personal and public appreciation for the Lord's blessings.

Individuals who become victim to their self-created fearful illusions have rarely considered where they are going, let alone how they might get there. As the old Talmudic saying goes, "If you don't know where you are going, any road will get you there." Such lost souls have no lofty goals, no elevated standards, and no aspirations beyond the self-interest and fear that drive their daily routine. They move without faith and spiritual understanding because there is none within them. They have no sure foundation on which to build their lives. Helaman taught: "And now, my sons, remember, remember that it is upon the rock of our Redeemer, who is Christ, the Son of God, that ye must build your foundation; that when the devil shall send forth his mighty winds, yea, his shafts in the whirlwind, yea, when all his hail and his mighty storm shall beat upon you, it shall have no power over you to drag you down to the gulf of misery and endless wo, because of the rock upon which ye are built, which is a sure foundation, a foundation whereon if men build they cannot fall" (Hel. 5:12).

It is in the constant effort to be better and to do better—living in, as far as is possible, the maximum of one's capabilities—that promotes increased faith and progress. Those who live in their fear are resigned to simply plod along. Sadly, they will continue blaming others for their own misfortunes, refusing to be responsible for their own actions. If we harbor doubt and distrust, we cannot dedicate ourselves to an elevated goal; we cannot move from where we are to where we *could be*.

In one of the case studies, there was a woman who, because she had had a terribly hard life, blindly followed what others dictated. She could not follow her own convictions because she lived in constant fear of making a mistake. She was left to travel through circuitous thorny thickets, listening only to what others opined. In times of crisis, she was left paralyzed, seeking counsel from this one or that one, tallying up the numbers until she arrived at a majority of opinions. She dared not follow her own convictions because if she were to make a mistake, she would have no one to blame but herself. Following the advice of her home teacher, her bishop, or even the stranger on the street allowed her to center blame on someone or something else. She was a martyr who fell prostrate before the golden calf of other's opinions, living a rudderless life.

She even censured God. *I don't know why God wanted me to marry that evil man*, she said, *but I did what I was told.* Once again, by blaming God, she was not at fault. She had sacrificed her divine right of agency, choosing instead to live in fear of making a mistake. Her fear had removed any faith in herself that she might once have had. Those who have no individual voice but only whimper out the thin echo of other's opinions are easily persuaded to useless battle as they struggle for more and more in their perceived life of scarcity.

Allow yourself the privilege of experiencing the beauty of the world. Don't allow someone else to make your crucial decisions. In addition, don't allow unwanted and unwarranted fear to ruin your faith in your decisions. Cultivate your faith. Recognize that in it rests the power to realize your dreams—your happiness. "Remember, the man who is to be pitied is the one who is sinking because he refuses to swim."

Man's fear is but a mortal illusion, and its deliverance comes from "another kind of fear—fearing" God (serving Him and keeping His commandments). If we righteously fear God, our faith will increase proportionately until one day we will come to know that there is nothing in this world we need to fear. He will make it so. For, as the Lord has promised, "Fear not, little flock; do good; let earth and hell combine against you, for if ye are built upon my rock, they cannot prevail" (D&C 6:34).

FAITH

Because faith is the opposite of fear, we can learn much about fear by better understanding faith. Faith is based on truth and precedes complete knowledge (we must learn all we can about the truth we seek if we are to have faith in it). While faith does not give a perfect knowledge, it does instill us with "hope for things which are not seen, which are true" (Alma

32:21). And when this hope leads us to believe in truths we cannot verify by scientific means, we gain spiritual knowledge and our faith is increased. When we add spiritual insight to our hopes and our (limited) knowledge, we can increase our knowledge and our faith many times over.

To acquire spiritual knowledge, with its preceding faith, one must do those things that are in tune with the Spirit. This is such a simple statement that its depth of meaning is often overlooked. For example, daily study of the scriptures (or other good books) can provide spiritual knowledge, but it is in doing what the scriptures instruct that spiritual knowledge is internalized, confirmed, and realized. Spiritually *knowing* but not *doing* makes the knowing somewhat irrelevant and could actually stand to condemn us in the last days—for we will be judged by what we know of God's laws. The Apostle James stated this principle boldly and simply: "Faith without works is dead" (James 2:20). So it is in the doing, and not just in the hearing, that one actively exercises faith. It is in the keeping of His commandments, not just in reading them, that our spiritual knowledge of these divine laws is able to transform us into an extension of His love and His power.

What happens, though, if we care more about listening than doing? A minister friend of mine, not a member of the Church, took a group of young people to a homeless shelter one Sunday morning to assist in preparing breakfast for those less fortunate. They had been there only an hour when the girls in the group asked to be excused to go home to get ready for church services. He responded with the question, "Would you prefer to actually help the poor or go to church and hear about helping the poor?" The sad part of this true tale is that the girls left in order to "keep the Sabbath holy." They did not yet understand and therefore did little that Sunday morning to increase their faith.

We increase our faith the same way we increase or develop any other skill. We study, we ponder, and we pray for something important— something that will assist our growth and understanding—and then we work at it. James questioned: "What doth it profit, my brethren, though a man say he hath faith and have not works? can faith save him? . . . Faith, if it hath not works, is dead, being alone. . . . For as the body without the spirit is dead, so faith without the spirit is dead also" (James 2:14, 16, 26). Increase your knowledge of the truth and you will increase your faith. Increase your faith and you will increase your knowledge. This is the key to overcome one's fear so as to overcome the grief that would otherwise accompany that fear. In the standard works, the phrase "fear not" appears a total of eighty-seven times. This is not by chance; we exist that we "might have joy" (2 Ne. 2:25). Fear not, and be happy.

Section Two

HOW TO INCREASE YOUR HAPPINESS

Chapter Ten
KNOWLEDGE BEYOND THE MIND

IN THE PREFACE, I MENTIONED that after the remarkable people in my case studies had achieved Kubler-Ross's final level of acceptance—when their self-inflicted grief had been subdued and a new peace and happiness had entered their lives, they found, as they expressed it, a higher level of understanding drifting into their lives, residing there for a time and then gradually retreating. They referred to this recurring experience as "knowledge beyond the mind." It seemed it was their reward for righteous living after having struggled so long to overcome their grief.

The purpose of this chapter is to have the reader understand how this spiritual knowledge beyond the mind works and how understanding it can help you to achieve your quest to find and enjoy an increased level of spiritual happiness. I will begin with a personal account that explains this phenomenon—a knowledge that exists beyond the mind.

When I was a young man, I went on a memorable date with the young woman who later became my wife. As we were driving around in our little farming community, I came to a non-gated railroad crossing. After looking both ways and seeing nothing, I started to go across the tracks when I had a strong prompting that I should stop the car. Without analyzing my feelings, I quickly slammed on the brakes and skidded to a halt. The next thing I knew, a blast of wind rocked my car as a speeding train roared by, narrowly missing the front bumper. Had I not paid attention to that whispering of the Spirit, we surely would have been killed. In that terrifying moment, my future wife was reduced to tears.

Of course, my conscious mind did nothing that night to save our lives. It couldn't because it didn't know that a massive train was speeding down the tracks in the dark of night. What I learned from that experience, and other similar experiences, is that an immeasurable amount of intelligence

(I call it spiritual understanding) exists beyond the knowledge of the mind. In comparison, our minds are puny and unreliable. But when we rely on the whisperings of the Spirit, as I did that night, truth is revealed. In that knowledge there are no doubts or anxieties. There is only assurance that it is true.

The knowledge we once had but is now forgotten is in the repository of our spiritual understanding. We may not remember our premortal lives, but we can still feel at least a sliver of truth without understanding why, or even how, we know something of divine origin to be true.[44] Recognizing truth as taught by the Spirit may come at a specific moment, as it did when I was "told" to stop before crossing the railroad tracks, but often it is simply a deeply felt conviction of something important. You don't know why you know, nor is it something you need to try to understand. You just feel that it is true in your mind and in your heart: "Yea, behold, I will tell you in your mind and in your heart, by the Holy Ghost, which shall come upon you and which shall dwell in your heart" (D&C 8:2). In this knowledge you will find the peace that makes life bearable—even enjoyable, although your world may be turned upside down. When we can't trust the mind alone to arrive at truth, we can always trust our spiritual understanding as received through the Holy Ghost and find therein the abiding faith to continue on.

My earliest recollection of spiritually knowing came in answer to a prayer when I was just a boy. My father, a farmer by trade, had left me with a big responsibility—to irrigate the fields next to the river. If the water was not turned off at the right moment, it would overflow and break through the bank. If that happened (as sad experience had taught), the water could wash away a portion of ground as big as a house down into the river in a matter of minutes.

While I knew the seriousness of my responsibility, it did not preclude me from playing with my cousin while waiting to change the water to the next dike. We used to take turns pitching my shovel (required to do the irrigation) high into the air, causing it to do a flip in midair before coming down and sticking into the ground without falling over. The one who got the best "stick" won the game.

One day, as the water neared the end of the levy, I pitched my shovel high into the air. When it came down, it was lost in the surrounding greasewoods. Hunt as we might, we could not find it. Time was against us. Without the shovel, I could not change the water, and much of the ground

---

44   See Richard Eyre, *Life before Life* (Salt Lake City: Deseret Book, 2000).

would be washed away. The water was rising, and in a few more minutes, it would be too late.

It was at that helpless moment that I felt a need to pray. I no sooner ended my prayer than I turned to my cousin, pointing at a large greasewood patch nearby, and said, "The shovel is over there." We ran to the patch and, sure enough, there was the shovel, perfectly stuck in the middle of the greasewood, blending in with the tall, thorny branches. That was the day my first prayer was answered. That was the day I first *spiritually knew* something that my mind did not and could not know.

I suspect you too have had promptings or spiritual communications of one kind or another, given specifically for your welfare. They exist in the absolute, as anyone who has experienced them will attest. They are not subject to man's rationalization or logic for their verification. As we follow the Spirit's instructions, the enticing illusions of the natural man automatically become progressively less attractive and alluring.

This reminds me of when my son Robert, as a two-year-old, developed double pneumonia and had to be hospitalized. We feared for his life, as did the doctors. One night, after playing for a dance at the local country club, I went to the hospital to visit him. As I leaned over the oxygen tent that shrouded his little crib at 2:00 a.m., I saw my little child trying desperately to breathe, panting rapidly like a baby rabbit. He looked to me with desperation on his tiny face as if he were to die at any moment. The scene brought fear to my heart. In my panic, I offered up the most sincere prayer I had ever uttered in my life. As I finished my petition, a feeling of peace swept over me. I had total knowledge (a spiritual understanding) that he was going to be made well. The next day, the doctor called to tell us that Robert's condition had greatly improved during the night and he was now out of danger. Of course, I already knew. I had been spiritually informed and could not deny it.

Brigham Young once asked, "How . . . are we to know the voice of the Good Shepherd from the voice of a stranger? Can any person answer this question?" To this, President Young answered definitively:

> I can. It is very easy. To every philosopher upon the earth,
> I say, your eye can be deceived, so can mine; your ear can
> be deceived, so can mine; the touch of your hand can be
> deceived, so can mine; but the Spirit of God filling the
> creature with revelation and the light of eternity, cannot
> be mistaken—the revelation which comes from God is

> never mistaken. . . . When an individual, filled with the
> Spirit of God, declares the truth of heaven, . . . the Spirit
> of the Lord pierces their inmost souls and sinks deep into
> their hearts; by the testimony of the Holy Ghost, light
> springs up within them, and they see and understand for
> themselves.[45]

Spiritual understanding is a gift given as an answer to prayer or as a divine response to a specific need that may or may not be requested or even known. It comes by way of inspired confirmation as truth is miraculously revealed. Gaining spiritual understanding with its accompanying happiness is a process in which we can grow progressively stronger. As we are inspired with one truth, for example, our search for additional light and knowledge is expanded because, as previously noted, all truths are circumscribed into one great whole. Line upon line, precept upon precept, we grow stronger in understanding, "for the Spirit speaketh the truth and lieth not" (Jacob 4:13). Thus, by accepting the first piece of this interwoven puzzle, we are led "line upon line, precept upon precept" (D&C 98:12) to other pieces that increase our spiritual understanding, our faith, and, lest we forget, our happiness.

This process also includes overcoming our trials and tribulations. Consider the old story of a farmer's donkey that fell into a shallow, old, dried-up well. The animal brayed pathetically for hours as the farmer tried to figure out what to do. He finally decided that since the animal was old and the well needed to be covered up anyway, it just wasn't worth the effort to try to save the donkey. He asked all his neighbors to come over and help him. They all grabbed their shovels and, digging furiously, began to throw dirt into the well. The donkey continued his pitiful braying. Then, to everyone's surprise, it quieted down. It seemed to be at peace with all that was happening. The farmer looked down the well and was astonished at what he saw. With every shovel of dirt that hit its back, the donkey would shake it off and take a step up. In spite of its predicament, the donkey was now at peace because it understood there was a way out. Pretty soon, the well was filled, and the donkey, stepping over the edge, trotted off.

Life is going to shovel dirt on us—all kinds of dirt. But when we spiritually understand and accept God's will, we too can find peace, shake it off, and step up. It is in this peace that we can understand that there is a God

---

45   *Journal of Discourses*, 16:75.

who loves us. And because of that love, we can spiritually know that there is a way out of the deepest "wells" of our lives. This is the understanding that came to those patients who, in this study, had accepted their troubles and were ready to move on.

If we succumb to the uncertainties of life, what we see merely reflects our own overriding fears of being buried by all of our problems. In our fear, we don't see things as they really are; we see them as *we* really are. That process is totally backward. We should first nurture our own spiritual knowledge, big or small, allowing that understanding to ever expand our faith and lead to more knowledge. Then, like the donkey, we will be able to shake off our troubles and step up to life's opportunities.

Somewhere in this process of life, we need to understand the difference between what our carnal mind says we need to be happy and what the Lord has said will contribute to our lasting peace and happiness. The things that matter most, revealed to us in scripture and spiritual understandings, do not have an expensive price tag. They are gifts given as a reward for obeying the Creator's governing laws. The cleaning label for the things of lasting value warns that they not be washed in "the ways of the world" but rather soaked in virtue, rinsed daily with good thoughts and repentance, dried in the warmth of the Son and the Father, and, above all, worn with love. These are the things we should strive to achieve if we are to build increased spiritual knowledge that exists beyond the carnal mind. Then we will recognize our divine heritage and act (and think) accordingly.

In "Concern for the One," Elder Joseph B. Wirthlin speaks of those who are spiritually lost, how they come to be lost, and what we can do to help them (or even ourselves) find spiritual understanding. To explain this, he recounts a tale from his youth. It seems that a fellow classmate who had difficulty walking and speaking was often teased and pushed around by other classmates—many of them Elder Wirthlin's own friends. This bothered young Elder Wirthlin greatly. He recounts:

> One day I could bear it no longer. Although I was only seven years old, the Lord gave me the courage to stand up to my friends.
>
> "Don't touch him," I said to them. "Stop teasing him. Be kind. He is a child of God!"
>
> My friends stepped back and turned away.
>
> I wondered at the time if my boldness would jeopardize my relationship with them. But the opposite happened.

> From that day onward, my friends and I became closer. They showed increased compassion for the boy. They became better human beings. To my knowledge, they never taunted him again.[46]

In a word, his friends had gained spiritual understanding. As you become aware of all the things that regularly happen in this creation of the Lord's, you will feel that it all takes place just for you. Being aware of His glorious gifts and goodness allows us to continually progress to ever-higher levels of spiritual consciousness and increased levels of happiness. When we know who we are in relationship to all that takes place in this universe, we can go beyond the mind to places where the natural man cannot go. It is in that spiritual understanding that we will refuse to pay homage to our pride but rather follow the simple rule to "love thy neighbor as thyself" (Matt. 22:39), for all are sons and daughters of our Heavenly Father.

It is sometimes difficult to grasp this spiritual understanding because we are so programmed to evaluate all things with the mind's logic. Many times, we fail to realize that our thoughts can only serve us well if we choose thoughts and actions that are confirmed by the Spirit, for it is only through the Spirit that we arrive at truth. As the Lord instructed, "My thoughts are not your thoughts, neither are your ways my ways. . . . For as the heavens are higher than the earth, so are my ways higher than your ways, and my thoughts than your thoughts" (Isa. 55:8–9).

If we learn to walk in His ways, then we will learn to spiritually understand His thoughts and His love for us. It is then that the unanswerable questions of the world are revealed as reasonable because they will have been explained by the Spirit. Even though our intellect may be a source of support, offering pertinent information to some of our inquiries, truth cannot be confirmed as truth until it is spiritually revealed. For "the Spirit manifesteth truth" (D&C 91:4), and "no man knoweth of His ways save it be revealed unto him; wherefore, brethren, despise not the revelations of God" (Jacob 4:8).

One may study and read about Christ's suffering in the Garden of Gethsemane and His Crucifixion, for example, but until the Spirit confirms the veracity of those events, they will simply remain narratives about the barbaric death of a great man who may or may not have existed. However, once the absolute truth and greatness of that singular event is revealed to man's spiritual understanding, the Savior's atoning sacrifice becomes not only logical but life changing. A true understanding of

---

46 "Concern for the One," *Ensign*, May 2008, 18.

the weight of His sacrifice and unconditional love for us then brings us to our knees in personal gratitude. In our quest for increased spiritual knowledge of what matters most, we should remember that it is not just how far down the path we travel, but also how many we help along the way. Once we stop relying solely on our own minds and open ourselves to the knowledge granted only through the Spirit, we will be that much more likely to overcome the sorrows and to embrace the joys of this life.

Chapter Eleven

LIVE IN THE NOW

WHILE I WAS STRUGGLING TO overcome my grief after Carolyn died, it suddenly occurred to me that just as past negative thoughts held me hostage in my grief, positive thoughts could free me. I also realized that this would all happen in the very moment of thinking about them. Obviously, the pain I felt with Carolyn's passing was not something I had felt in the past or would feel in the future; it was an experience for the present moment—the *now*. This realization produced one of those "aha" moments in my life that, for whatever reason, I don't normally pay a lot of attention to. However, if we look at this one more closely, it is easy to see its importance.

One of my dear friends experienced a lower brain aneurism. While the doctors were able to save his life, he no longer has the ability to walk and struggles to communicate as well as eat. When I visit him, I spend my time talking about the good old days on the farm. As I recount special events he and I experienced together, I watch with joy as his eyes light up with this or that story. And if the story is good enough, he will laugh with excitement as his mind takes him back to that very occasion. He may be revisiting joy of moments past, but he actually experiences that joy in the present.

For example, can you look out the window from where you are at this precise moment and see something wonderful? You can, for almost everything in nature offers something beautiful. The majestic clouds rolling in on a stormy or sunny day (it doesn't matter which), birds flying in a blue sky, plants growing from seeds previously sown or scattered by the wind, the sun, the moon, the stars, the birth of anything—all these things and more declare the magnificence of God's creation and His love. But we can appreciate all of them and more only in the present moment. We cannot appreciate them yesterday or tomorrow but only today. Happiness, much like grief, comes only to us in the now.

The negative power of the mind, however, lives mainly in the past because that is where it gets its negative "food for thought." But just as bad memories and grief always travel together, happy thoughts and feelings of tranquility also travel together.

When you understand there is nothing in your past or your future that can stop you from saying yes to what is in this moment, you will find the connection to how thoughts can govern happiness. Then you will experience all of the good around you—good that exists in abundance.

I began to practice this procedure of living in the now about a year after Carolyn's death. It didn't take me long to realize that the Lord's creations exist for our enjoyment. I learned to reverence things that heretofore went by my "window" of life without consideration. For instance, I recently accompanied my son Steven in his small airplane on a business trip. As the plane lifted off the runway, I was focused on all of the fascinating things happening in that moment to cause a heavy piece of metal to fly through the air with the greatest of ease.

A few minutes later, when we suddenly broke through the clouds, I saw one of the most beautiful sights of my life. There, underneath us, were high mountains and deep valleys of billowy white clouds arrayed in beautiful formation. While not as detailed and colorful as the fall leaves of the trees on the mountains, they were, nevertheless, breathtaking. The rising sun gave added color and dimension to the scene's brilliant radiance and magnificence. I was in awe!

There was no grief in that remarkable moment—nor could there be, for I had learned not to dwell on the past or the future (at least no more than was warranted for practical purposes)—for the present moment was all I had, and it was a moment I valued. Just remember, there is a good reason why the windshield in your car is many times bigger than the rearview mirror. We need to be looking out at what is there right now and not gazing endlessly into the small mirror at what is behind us. Following that practice keeps us safe, both while driving and while navigating through life.

If you have to call on the past or the future, don't stay long. Do what you need to do and then get back to the present. That is where your life is glorified. That is where you can handle any present pain with the understanding that "this too shall pass." To call forth additional pain and grief from the negative memory bank of the past is foolish—yet we unconsciously do it much of the time. My suggestion is to "wake up and smell the roses" or anything else that smells nice—now!

The harder we try to put sadness behind us by reviewing past events in a negative light, the more it takes center stage. But the more we focus on things outside of our own misery (things that give us joy right now), the more predominant they become, and they brighten our day. Remember that when I was mired in my grief, I pushed harder for some resolution, reviewing over and over in my mind my "unsolvable" problems and increasing my grief. But then, with a little shift of emphasis away from those thoughts, I became more aware of the ebb and flow of the joy around me. I learned that all things in God's creation could speak to me. I stopped my negative thinking and waited patiently for a new season to brighten my life with its snow or its thaw—it didn't matter which.

When the Prophet Joseph Smith was suffering horribly in Liberty Jail, the Lord lovingly counseled, "My son, peace be unto thy soul; thine adversity and thine afflictions shall be but a small moment; And then, if thou endure it well, God shall exalt thee on high; thou shalt triumph over all thy foes" (D&C 121:7–8). The Lord didn't say, "Peace be unto your soul *tomorrow*." Nor did He say, "My peace was unto you *last week*." When God said, "Peace be unto thy soul," Joseph felt immediate peace despite all that was happening to him. And I don't doubt that that peace stayed with him in the present moment of every day. All he had to do was think of that blessing in order to experience a moment of peace in his now.

Consider the story of a schoolteacher who asked her students to write down what they thought were the Seven Wonders of the World. After the students turned in their assignments, these were their top seven: Egypt's great pyramids, the Taj Mahal, the Great Canyon, the Panama Canal, the Empire State Building, St. Peter's Basilica, and the Great Wall of China. But one girl was reluctant to turn in her list because hers were different. Her seven wonders included the abilities to see, hear, touch, taste, feel, laugh, and love.

As the teacher read aloud this student's list to her fellow classmates, the room became quiet. The girl had bypassed the "things" of the world and had gone directly to its real wonders. She had listened to her heart and found the Creator of the universe speaking to her. If you listen carefully, you too can hear Him speak to you. And all of these gifts are available to you right now—in the present.

This seems like such a simple concept, but having such things testify or speak to me was a relatively new experience. This came to me little by little as I too became more aware of the spiritual aspect of life. Not just man's spirit, but the spirits of all things—for all things were first created spiritually: "For I, the Lord God, created all things, of which I have spoken, spiritually, before they were naturally upon the face of the earth" (Moses 3:5).

In this process of gaining increased spiritual awareness, I learned that I was not as alone as I had supposed. In reality, I was never alone, but I didn't know it because I had not paid attention to the things around me. Silence now comforts me like an old friend. The morning breeze from my patio speaks to me with its reassuring sighs. The sun, moon, and stars have all become more relevant to me than ever before because they testify of God's existence and of His love for me. I now take notice of the smallest things. Each tells me about its divine creation and whispers of eternity. Each speaks to me with the profound love and understanding offered so unconditionally by the Lord. Each teaches me that I am secure and in a safe place, regardless of what is happening out there in my "other" world. Each draws me out of my self-centered misery into a world created for you and me that has peace and calm as its foundation, a world that is my retreat in an otherwise noisy existence.

As I look at these marvelous things around me, I begin to understand God's abundance. I listen to soft music. How absolutely wonderful is that? I am fine. I see nature outside my window. The world is fine. It is in this setting that I find contentment, which comes only in experiencing the now.

Thoughts on the theatrical stage of the mind come and go. But unlike the local theater attractions, what's playing on your stage depends entirely on you. If you want to be engaged in something creative and inspiring, that program is ready and waiting for you. But remember, you must carefully choose and protect the top billing you give certain thoughts and ideas because they can change in a split second. It is up to you to determine what they are. You have power over your destiny because you have power over your thoughts . . . and, as you know, your destiny is, in large part, the result of your thoughts. Carefully selected thoughts of what is taking place right now in your world can be of much more value to you than your mind's random thoughts of the past or future.

As you light your marquee with what's showing today, keep in mind there is a direct correlation between what's playing and what's happening to you or for you. If your stage depicts negative, judgmental thoughts or acts of vengeful anger or indifference or even portrays you acting with a sense of demanding false pride, then all of these scenes will surely *become* you unless you produce a new and a more wisely conceived coming attraction. As long as we are engaged in a cause of rightness, our thoughts will always lead us to that special "epic" engagement, and we will not have to worry about what's playing at the other local theaters. Just as we can never ascend higher than our thoughts, we will never descend lower than where they have taken us. Therefore, we need to listen carefully to the promptings of the Spirit as we read, meditate, ponder, and pray. As we do so, we will replace the illusions generated by the natural man with the truths of the Spirit.

As I find myself becoming more and more balanced in my thoughts, I see that God provides for my every need, even my need to experience opposition. I just needed to be present to see it. What I was looking for (how to overcome my own grief and find happiness) was already there as I moved from the painful memories of the past toward the uplifting reality of the present. I feel as if I have entered a new life—one filled with His love and acceptance. Now as I gaze out, I whisper to myself, "What could be more illogical than to resist something this beautiful?" I now resolve that I will never resist what is, even the death of a loved one, ever again. This because I have truly come to understand that "all these things shall give [me] experience, and shall be for [my] good" (D&C 122:7).

Remember, however, that it makes no sense to focus on the present if all you look for is the negative. If you are driving down the road looking for inconsiderate drivers, for example, you are certain to find them. But if you focus on finding the beauty of the world on the "freeway of life"— including the existence of the Savior and His atoning sacrifice—your life will be filled will joy that will gradually—sometimes even immediately— overcome any sorrow.

Awhile back I traveled with a friend and his wife to another city. They dropped me off at the appointed place and time where my wife was to meet me to take me the rest of the way home. Because my wife was lost in her own "present moment," she arrived late. While waiting, I took the occasion to wander through the parking lot. There I found the most beautiful antique convertible I believe I have ever seen. I systematically walked around it several times, admiring the craftsmanship and the owner's careful efforts to restore and care for it. It brought back fond memories of the little convertible I'd once had when I was in college. Just seeing that car brought me joy.

As I looked around at some of the buildings on the street, I reveled in the detail and the design of each. I saw an old barbershop with a faded American flag hanging outside. There was a big multicolored pinwheel spinning in the gentle breeze. Alongside it was an old, faded sign that read, "Have You Thanked a Vet Today?" At that moment, I wished I had more time to wander, for I would have liked to have had my hair cut there just for the experience. But, alas! My wife arrived, begging my forgiveness for being late. Did I care? Of course not! I was too caught up in the joys of the moment to have minded. I had expanded my joy by focusing on the positive aspects of the present. As the Lord revealed to the Saints of this dispensation, "He who receiveth all things with thankfulness shall be made glorious; and the things of this earth shall be added unto him, even an hundred fold, yea, more" (D&C 78:19).

I have heard evangelists preach the law of expansion, saying that it will bring to us anything we desire—riches, power, health—and that it can do so now. While I believe that a law of expansion exists, my belief is somewhat different from what many of the evangelists advocate. If you are kind, for example, kind people will be attracted to you and you to them—and that kindness will expand. If by your nature you are loving, others who are loving will be attracted to you and you to them—and that love will expand. If you find harmony and patience in your conscious mind, that too will be reflected in your daily living—and that too will expand. If you align your thoughts and actions with God's, those thoughts and actions will also attract His blessings, and they will expand.

The law of attraction begins in the conscious mind—but it offers no one a free ride. To make it work, you must be there—in the present moment. The bride may happily look forward to her marriage tomorrow, for example, but her happiness is experienced in the moment, in the anticipation of tomorrow. Tomorrow she will experience that joy again in a more direct way but only when tomorrow is today. You too can experience happiness but only when you are present and only in the now.

If you are irritated and impatient, revisiting some moment of anger, sadness, or recent drama in your life, do what President Dieter F. Uchtdorf instructed and just stop![47] If you don't, you are only inviting your grief to increase. Since pain can only feed on pain, don't feed it! Let it starve. Don't ignore or deny yourself the pleasure of the present moment because that is where happiness is found. You can only be happy now, not yesterday or tomorrow. Only when tomorrow is today can you be happy. Realize that the present moment is all you have.

---

47   "The Merciful Obtain Mercy," *Ensign*, May 2012.

Everything that happens or that will ever happen, happens in the now. And if you do it right, nurturing proper thoughts now and acting accordingly, you will be carried away from the cares of the world and will overcome those trials that would otherwise be stressful experiences. As the early Saints of our day sang, "Why should we think to earn a great reward If we now shun the fight?" ("Come, Come, Ye Saints," *Hymns*, no. 30). Don't shun the fight; embrace it. Now.

Chapter Twelve
INCREASE YOUR LOVE
AND CHANGE YOUR WORLD

FOR ME, THERE WERE THREE big (I might even say gigantic) surprises that came out of my research. The first was that in our innocence, we are often guilty of embracing those things that either cause us grief, sustain it, or increase it. We now know some of the reasons as to why this takes place. The second surprise was that those who overcome their grief find there is a spiritual knowledge that exists beyond the mind (even Kubler-Ross didn't know that). The third discovery, equally as surprising as the other two (and the topic for this chapter), was the occurrence of a notable positive shift in attitude and character after emerging victorious from grief. In following the people in the study, I found that not only did most of these patients have a renewed love and appreciation for life, but they were also more kind and caring for others than they had been in the past. As they increased their love for others, they changed their world. To illustrate how this shift comes about, let me tell you a true story.

My son Scott hired a repairman to do some work at his house. When the man arrived, Scott, in his singularly outgoing manner, happily asked the man how he was doing. The man replied, "Well, on a scale of one to ten, I'm about a twenty." He went on to explain that for years he had been suffering from a degenerative heart disease. After a few years of unsuccessful treatment, the doctors told him the only thing that could save his life was a heart transplant. In the final stages of the disease, he was finally approved as a recipient, and after anxiously waiting for several weeks, a donor was found. The operation was successful and . . . the rest is history. He said he would never again take his life for granted. He was happy all the time, determined to never let anything bother him. It changed his appreciation for life, and it changed the way he treated others. He reached out to everyone, including strangers, bringing them into his circle of love. His kindness was contagious, and why not? Love does, indeed, beget love.

What happens to so many of those who overcome grief is not just the emergence of appreciation for a life that many thought they were going to lose. It is a spiritual shift to those things that matter most—great things—like the love of God. That kind of love is confirmed in the scriptures as the great commandment. Remember what Christ taught: "And, behold, a certain lawyer stood up, and tempted him, saying, Master, what shall I do to inherit eternal life? . . . And he answering said, Thou shalt love the Lord thy God with all thy heart, and with all thy soul, and with all thy strength, and with all thy mind; and thy neighbour as thyself" (Luke 10:25, 27).

God has commanded us to love Him and our neighbors as ourselves because all things good flow into and out of love. Recognize that you cannot truly love without having charity. You cannot truly love without being kind. You cannot truly love without being humble. You cannot truly love without being appreciative of your blessings. But it works both ways. You cannot truly have charity for others and not have love. You cannot genuinely be kind to others and not have love. You cannot truly be humble and not have love. You cannot be appreciative and not have love. This takes place because, again, all things are circumscribed into one great whole. And that whole is love—the subject of the greatest commandment of all.

In speaking of the pure love of Christ, often referred to as charity, the Apostle Paul wrote, "Though I speak with the tongues of men and of angels, and have not charity, I am become as sounding brass, or a tinkling cymbal" (1 Cor. 13:1). Of this scripture, Elder Joseph B. Wirthlin said, "Paul's message to this new body of Saints was simple and direct: Nothing you do makes much of a difference if you do not have charity. You can speak with tongues, have the gift of prophecy, understand all mysteries, and possess all knowledge; even if you have the faith to move mountains, without charity it won't profit you at all."[48]

How to Change Your World

As you increase your love for others, you will begin to change your world for the better. But how to truly love is somewhat vague and is certainly subject to interpretation. And while there are many worthwhile characteristics that lead to love, there is need for a specific formula that will teach us how to love—one that has been tested and proven to bring the desired results we want, one that's easy to understand, easy to follow, and that, without fail, will lead us to increased love. Incidentally, as our level of love is increased, so is the level of our spirituality. To increase one is to increase the other.

---

48 "The Great Commandment," *Ensign*, November 2007, 28.

In his insightful and inspiring book *Transcending Levels of Consciousness: The Stairway to Enlightenment*, David Hawkins tells us how to increase our spirituality and therefore our love. He states, "[One] tried-and-true basic tool that has brought about tremendous results over the centuries [is to] *be kind to everything and everyone, including oneself, all the time, with no exceptions.*"[49]

There you have it—a simple, straightforward formula that has been tested over the centuries and is easy to understand and follow. Simply be kind to everything and everyone, including oneself, all the time, with no exceptions, and your love and level of spirituality will increase.

Let's look at the formula more closely. What does it mean to be kind to everything? Should we be kind to the earth? Absolutely. What about the plants? Of course. What about the insects? Why not? After all, they are literally part of God's creation. Take a look at how the book of Moses describes this: "For I, the Lord God, created all things, of which I have spoken, spiritually, before they were naturally upon the face of the earth. . . . And out of the ground made I, the Lord God, to grow every tree, naturally, that is pleasant to the sight of man; and man could behold it. *And it became also a living soul. For it was spiritual in the day that I created it*; for it remaineth in the sphere in which I, God, created it, yea, even all things which I prepared for the use of man" (Moses 3:5–9; emphasis added). This is certainly good news for those of us who like to talk to our plants.

In 1835, the book of Abraham came to light when an ancient Egyptian papyrus was discovered and Joseph Smith translated it. It likewise chronicles the Creation of the world. The amazing thing is that these two ancient books, Moses and Abraham, though obtained in different ways from unrelated sources and translated and recorded at separate times in ancient history, are mutually collaborative. Compare, if you will, what is stated in Abraham 4:12 to what we have read in Moses: "And the Gods organized the earth to bring forth grass from its own seed, and the herb to bring forth herb from its own seed, yielding seed after his kind; and the earth to bring forth the tree from its own seed, yielding fruit, whose seed could only bring forth the same in itself, after his kind; and the Gods saw that they were obeyed."

What was to obey the Gods? The grass, the herbs, and the trees. This revealing explanation confirms that these plants have a living spirit—the same as you and I—albeit less intelligent. Therefore, when the grass, the herbs, and the trees were commanded to reproduce and bring forth from

---

49　"Simple Tools for Great Value," ConsiousnessProject.org, 2009, http://consciousnessproject.org/articles/simple-tools-of-great-value/.

their own seed, they did so, following their own DNA. To reinforce this concept, in verse 18, it reiterates, "And the Gods watched those things which they had ordered until they obeyed." To obey a command, the grass, the herbs, and the trees had to be intelligent enough to "understand" what they were being told to do and have the capacity to do it. Since we have the same capacity to understand and obey God, should we be less than the plants? I think not.

In understanding that all things have a spirit, we are better able to comprehend miracles, for when spirit speaks to spirit, miraculous occurrences can take place. Remember what happened when Christ spoke to the elements? "And, behold, there arose a great tempest in the sea, insomuch that the ship was covered with the waves: but he was asleep. And his disciples came to him, and awoke him, saying, Lord, save us: we perish. And he saith unto them, Why are ye fearful, O ye of little faith? Then he arose, and rebuked the winds and the sea; and there was a great calm" (Matt. 8:24–26). Christ spoke to the wind and the sea, *spirit to spirit*, and there was great calm.

We need to be kind to everything without exception because we live in a spiritual world with spiritual connectedness. But the human mind often fails to understand this. What the mind often submits to is the disconnected, delusional ego. But if you bypass the ego-mind, you will be able to see clearly.

You don't have to be a hopeless victim of "spiritual blindness." If you know your spiritual eyesight is poor and think you can't do anything about it, you may go through life with clouded vision. But if you have the right prescription, your "corrective lenses" can miraculously make clear your distorted vision. Think and do those things that are compatible with the spirit—your divine prescription—and you will see clearly, thus subduing the ego.

Dale Tingey, former executive director of the American Indian Services and a friend of mine, spent a major portion of his life helping Native Americans in need of assistance. He has a great love for these people. I was honored to serve on his local board, which sponsors the Johnny Miller Invitational Golf Tournament in St. George each year to raise scholarship money for worthy Native American students. As one who has changed his world for the better, he is a model for those of us who would change our own world. He recently sent me the following inspiring words that were written on the tomb of an Anglican bishop (1100 AD) in the crypts of Westminster Abbey.

When I was young and free and my imagination had no limits, I dreamed of changing the world. As I grew older and wiser, I discovered the world would not change, so I shortened my sights somewhat and decided to change only my country.

But it, too, seemed immovable.

As I grew into my twilight years, in one last desperate attempt, I settled for changing only my family, those closest to me, but alas, they would have none of it.

And now as I lie on my deathbed, I realize: If I had only changed myself first, then by example I would have changed my family. From their inspiration and encouragement, I would then have been able to better my country and, who knows, I may have even changed the world.

As you are freed from the ties that bind (and blind) you to only see things from a mortal perspective, you begin the quest to change your world through kindness. Since kindness is contagious, others will soon begin to change their worlds. If you are looking for purpose in your life, be kind to everything and everyone, including yourself. Make that your quest, and you and others around you will change for the better because of it.

Chapter Thirteen
MAKE THE "KIND" CONNECTION

SOME OF YOU MAY THINK that being kind to everything and everyone, including yourself, all the time, with no exceptions, would be a nice thing but perhaps not all that important. The truth is that it is very important because kindness and love are inseparable, and, as we've discussed, love is the essence of the greatest commandment. To speak of one is to speak of the other.

As a spiritual truth, kindness is interconnected with other spiritual truths. As you achieve one, you are automatically connected to others. This great connection takes place because, by logical definition, kindness is a fundamental truth upon which other truths are founded and from which they spring. Being kind is the seed for developing numerous virtues, not the least of which is love. If you want to increase your love for others (or the love that you want to receive from others), you must first be genuinely kind. As you do so, you will see that kindness is the principle way of growing love.

Some people turn inward, using kindness as a selfish "return on investment" in order to win friends, influence people, or to become popular. Others focus outward, having no thought of what the investment of effort might yield them personally. These, then, are the individuals who embody charity, the somewhat forgotten Christian characteristic.

To show how being kind links with other desirable characteristics, I will describe six common connections (out of the many that could be cited) that grow from someone being kind. These six connections, as well as their resulting growth, will demonstrate why it is important to be kind to everyone, including ourselves, and to do it without exception.

LOVE GROWS FROM KINDNESS

As previously mentioned, when one is kind to others for the right reasons, love grows. It is difficult to see kindness expressed anywhere without also seeing evidence of love. As kindness fills one's being, selfish attitudes and judgments are more easily purged and washed away. As kindness fills someone with love, that person becomes more compassionate as another connection takes place. As that person's love grows, so does understanding, forming another connection as old attitudes and habits of the natural man become less interesting. Such a person's new loving nature will overcome their deficiencies. And all of this springs from being kind.

But just as love builds, hate destroys. The absence of love is the foundation for hate. Therefore, the true constant in our life for peace and happiness must be our love and the love of God the Father and His Only Begotten Son. This love is best expressed with kindness. This higher law elicits new behavior and asks for "a new heart and a new spirit" (Ezek. 18:31), for love carries great expectations.

In his book *How to Pray for Lost Loved Ones*, author Dutch Sheets tells of how lecturer "Leo Buscaglia once talked about a contest he was asked to judge. The purpose of the contest was to find the most caring child. The winner was a four-year-old boy whose next-door neighbor was an elderly gentleman who had recently lost his wife. Upon seeing the man cry, the little boy . . . climbed onto his lap and just sat there. When his mother asked him what he had said to the neighbor, the boy said, 'Nothing. I just helped him cry.'"[50]

To give love, be kind. To receive love, be kind.

MEEKNESS SPRINGS FROM KINDNESS

Meekness, like love, is best reflected in acts of kindness. A meek man is a kind man. It cannot be otherwise. Meekness is best expressed as being teachable, which requires a certain submissiveness. Meekness opens the door to understanding the weightier matters that Christ alluded to when He said, "Take my yoke upon you, and learn of me." Then, as if to clarify, He said, "For I am meek and lowly in heart" (Matt. 11:29). If we are to take Christ's yoke upon us, we must be like Him. Since Christ was meek and lowly in heart, He was teachable and submissive to the Father and the Holy Ghost. Hence, would it not profit us even more to be meek and lowly in heart—to be more teachable and submissive? Think of all the things we might learn if we were open to that learning. We must be "easy to be entreated" (Alma 7:23) in order to learn.

The road to the gift of meekness is to work on becoming more kind to others, entreating the Lord for assistance in this worthy goal. Being kind,

---

50   *How to Pray for Lost Loved Ones* (Ventura, CA: Regal Books, 2001), 8.

especially to those who profess to be our enemies, can be terribly difficult. But as you reach out to others, you will learn of their trials and suffering and thus become more teachable.

In his article "Meekness—A Dimension of True Discipleship," Elder Neal A. Maxwell explained other benefits of meekness:

> Meekness can also help us in coping with the injustices of life—of which there are quite a few. . . .
>
> Besides, there can be dignity even in silence, as was the case when Jesus meekly stood, unjustly accused, before Pilate. . . . Holding back can be the sign of great personal discipline, especially when everyone else is letting go.
>
> Furthermore, not only are the meek less easily offended, but they are less likely to give offense to others. In contrast, there are some in life who seem, perpetually, to be waiting to be offended.
>
> Meekness also cultivates in us a generosity in viewing the mistakes and imperfections of others.[51]

Christ's statement, "Blessed are the meek, for they shall inherit the earth," is clear and concise—unless we are fooled by the world's perception of meekness. By the world's definition, *meekness* seems to connote *weakness*. Elder Maxwell wryly noted, "We even make nervous jokes about meekness, such as 'If the meek intend to inherit the earth, they are going to have to be more aggressive about it!'"[52]

Because the great power of meekness is not well understood or embraced, rarely do we think of a powerful leader as being meek. How many businesses have you heard of that give The Most Meek of the Year Award? None, I would venture. Yet the prophets have consistently warned that only the meek and lowly of heart are acceptable before God. If we could but believe in the reality of such revelatory statements, our mortal behavior would change. Elder Maxwell also stated, "You live in coarsening times, times in which meekness is misunderstood and even despised. Yet meekness has been, is, and will remain a non-negotiable dimension of true discipleship."[53]

Meekness holds the power not to forgive only sometimes but to forgive "seventy times seven" (Matt. 18:21–22). What better example of kindness is

---

51 "Meekness—A Dimension of True Discipleship," *Ensign*, March 1983, 70.

52 Ibid.

53 Ibid.

there than that? The meek are those who not only endure the animosity of their enemies but who also pray for them and love them (see Matt. 5:44). Meekness begins with the simple practice of being kind. Like love, meekness is a prerequisite for all else that is good.

GENTLENESS SPRINGS FROM KINDNESS

I recently attended the funeral of a dear, kind man who, by any criteria, was considered successful. Every morning he would walk the floor of his chemical company, shake the hands of his employees, and convey his appreciation to each. His kind manner was an expression of his absolute love. Upon his death, a flood of letters and telegrams arrived from former employees, supply-house agents, and clients—even though he had sold the business many years prior and had long since moved to a different state. I listened in awe as testimony after testimony was read at his funeral—tributes from a variety of associates from different areas. The central theme was always that he was a gentle man, a man of great love and compassion. The more I listened, the more I understood that his gentleness was the result of his being kind to all. What's more, it was key to his success.

A gentle person is easy to be with and easy to trust because he or she has no guile or conceit (the opposite characteristics of the egotistical natural man). One who is of a gentle nature obviously does not believe in violence except in cases of desperate self-defense and the defense of others. If gentle individuals ever have the need to correct someone, they will do so in a kind manner, as that is their defining characteristic.

Gentle people are neither insincere nor pushy—the latter of which is an exhausting and typically useless activity. Everyone is drawn to gentle people, for in them is safety and peace. They are never unkind or crude in speech or demeanor. The aim of gentle individuals is not to be better than someone else but only to become better themselves—gently.

Born in Germany but later emigrating to the United States, Dr. Constantine Hering, a pioneer of homeopathic medicine, lived by the motto *"Die milde Macht ist gross,"* or "The force of gentleness is great." If you are kind to others, you will become gentle, a characteristic worthy of your pursuit.

MERCY SPRINGS FROM KINDNESS

We who have our own final judgment in mind know that the greatest gift we could ever hope for is God's mercy. In His kind mercy, we will find relief from mistakes, sorrow, pain, damaged relationships, and, in short, everything troubling or vexing.

It is through Christ's merciful Atonement that our mistakes are made into something positive, becoming part of the learning process and not part of a disparaging degeneration. His mercy allows us to be forgiven and healed. In the words of a hymn, "Earth has no sorrow that heav'n cannot heal" ("Come, Ye Disconsolate," *Hymns*, no. 115). Through His mercy, the purpose of life is made whole. Without His kindness and His forgiveness, there would be nothing we could accomplish or pursue. As President Joseph F. Smith wrote, "But for the precious assurance and glorious hope in the Gospel of Christ, life would not only *not* be worth the living, but it would be an infamous and damning *farce!*"[54] Without the Atonement, life would be meaningless because mercy cannot rob justice (see Alma 42:25). To mortal man, His kind mercy shines forth in brilliant splendor because of its eternal consequence.

FORGIVENESS SPRINGS FROM KINDNESS

If we are kind to others, we must be forgiving, for that is the kindest thing we can ever do. Forgiveness requires mercy, which we just discussed. Forgiveness is Godlike in nature but human centered in action.

When we forgive the petty flaws of others, we have discharged ourselves from bondage, freeing the mind and spirit because forgiveness purifies the mind as well as the soul and is, perhaps, the deepest expression of kindness there is.

A critical and judgmental attitude chains one to the past, precluding one's capacity to enjoy the present or anticipate the joy of the future. Forgiveness allows one to break those chains and to have renewed hope in the present and future. It is in merciful forgiveness that one finds peace.

When I was recovering from my painful, invasive cancer treatments, no one ever criticized my sometimes less-than-laudable attitude. Without exception, those around me were forgiving and kind, often beyond what I deserved. They were sensitive to my pain and suffering, extending to me their support and love without thought of judgment, regardless of my intermittently irritable behavior. Their mercy, like their love, was unconditional.

Why, then, are we not as forgiving and merciful to those who are recovering from the "surgery of the soul" as we are to those who are recovering from

---

54 *Teachings of the Presidents of the Church: Joseph F. Smith* (Salt Lake City: The Church of Jesus Christ of Latter-day Saints,), 86.

the surgery of the body? Just because we do not see them confined to hospital beds or attached to life-support systems does not mean their condition is not critical. On such occasions, should we not be forgiving, since we too have experienced the pain and suffering of an ailing soul? Should we not have total empathy? A spiritual affliction is much more serious than any physical ailment we could have.

When Jesus was criticized for supping with unpopular tax collectors and sinners, He declared, "They that are whole have no need of the physician, but they that are sick: I came not to call the righteous, but sinners to repentance" (Mark 2:17). He also said, "Be ye therefore merciful, as your Father also is merciful" (Luke 6:36).

GRATITUDE SPRINGS FROM KINDNESS

The wise poet John Donne once wrote, "No man is an island entire of itself; every man is a piece of the continent, a part of the main. . . . And therefore never send to know for whom the bell tolls; it tolls for thee."[55] In the grandest sense of kindness, the recipient of kindness is not the only one who benefits. Just as we are indebted each day to thousands for the comforts, joys, and blessings of life, let us realize it is only by extending gratitude that we can begin to repay the debt to many. Only then can we begin to comprehend the importance of making gratitude the focus of all our living and a constant expression in outward acts rather than just an occasional thought.

APPRECIATION SPRINGS FROM KINDNESS

My first memory of receiving appreciation from others came when I was just a boy. At that time, my mother was president of our ward's Relief Society. As such, it was her task to distribute food to the needy of our small ward. Each week we would crank up our old truck, load it with food donated from the bishops' storehouse, and make our weekly run. Mom would drive the truck to a designated house. I would lug the large food basket to the front door, set it down, knock, and, without waiting, run like the wind back to the truck before anyone answered the door.

We didn't fool the people we were helping—at least not all of them. I knew that because on one occasion, while Mom and I were at the post

---

55 "Meditation XVII," in *Devotions Upon Emergent Occasions: Together with Death's Duel* (Middlesex: Echo Library, 2008), 97.

office, one of the women on our food run saw my mother. Without a word, she came over to Mom, put her arms around her, and began to cry. She never said a word—she just cried softly. Mom held her tightly until her sobs died down. "Just know we love you," Mom said quietly. The woman, wiping at her tears, smiled briefly and walked away. That woman taught me the greatest lesson on true gratitude I have ever received. And she did it without saying a word—and it all took place because we were kind to her.

Every kind deed to others is a great energy that starts an unending "ripple effect" through time and eternity. We may not notice it. We may never receive a word of gratitude or recognition for our efforts, but it will all come back to us in some form—as naturally, perfectly, and inevitably as an echo to the sender. It may not happen how we expect it to or when we expect it to, but sometime, somehow, somewhere, it will come back. Alma, when rebuking Corianton, his wayward son, said, "For that which ye do send out shall return unto you again, and be restored; therefore, the word restoration more fully condemneth the sinner, and justifieth him not at all" (Alma 41:15). So we must keep a close eye on what we "send out" into the world because it will be restored to us for our good or for our condemnation.

Prior to Carolyn's death, I hosted a party for her at our home. Most of the guests were friends we had not seen for a long time. Since she and I were the connecting link to the others who did not know each other, I took the occasion to comment on how we had become acquainted with each couple. I soon found I could not properly introduce them to each other without expressing appreciation for the things they had done for us. After I had finished these introductions, each couple in turn asked if they too might share their thoughts and feelings.

One man whom I had not seen in thirty years told the group how I had impacted the life of one of his sons. I am reluctant to tell you precisely what he said because it sounds so self-serving. But the story does illustrate the importance of being kind. It seems the boy had become a bit worldly in his teenage years—smoking and drinking, among other things. According to his father, I had, in some direct way, influenced him to change for the better so that eventually he could go on a mission. When this same boy, now a man with his own children, learned that his father and mother were going to be with us at this minireunion, he specifically told his father to thank me for what I had done. He said that because of my kindness to him, he had turned his life around. The interesting thing was that I didn't remember what I had done for him, but I will always remember how his father, mother, and others in the group impacted my life with their kindness. Indeed, we are all connected in all things. And what forges the links in all such beneficial connections is our ability to be kind to one another.

There is nothing unique or hidden about how being kind directly connects to a multitude of other worthwhile characteristics. Just as I selected a few by way of demonstration, you too could easily generate your own additional list of any number of characteristics that connect to kindness. As I stated before, all truths are circumscribed into one great whole. Each day, focus on being kind, and as one connection is made, goodness will ripple outward. When someone does something kind to you, be sure to pay it forward. In these ways, you can change your world— and others'.

Chapter Fourteen

GODLY PEACE:
THE HAPPINESS OF SPIRITUAL REALITY

As I MENTIONED AT THE beginning of the previous chapter, there were three big surprises that came out of this research. What I did not tell you was there were also four significant stages that were equally important to the development of this book. The first stage I call the Exploratory Stage. Were it not for the help of many giving people, I doubt I would have discovered that we can, and often do, create much of our own grief. The second stage is the Development Stage. It was here that the governing principles started to emerge, allowing me (and others like me) to stop creating our grief. The third stage is the Graduation Stage. It was here that I applied the practical and spiritual things I had learned from others, proving to me that they were valid. The fourth and final stage is the Reward Stage. In these stages, I experienced the full spectrum of emotions—going from self-imposed grief to self-generated spiritual happiness.

For those who want to complete the same journey, I explain some things in these last chapters that you can't anticipate—things that will probably surprise you and will certainly make you happy. Here is what I believe will happen, as stated before: As you consistently apply the principles of being kind, as described in the previous chapters, you will find increased clarity of mind. Rising above the clamor of the world, you will feel at peace. Because of the love you are giving by being kind to everything and everyone, including yourself, all of the time, with no exceptions, you will often find yourself becoming the patient observer, as it were, witnessing all that is going on without making unrighteous judgments. Because love begets love, the Lord will bless you with a spiritual level of understanding. During those moments, you will know why things are happening as they are. In this peaceful state, you will become untroubled by the frustrating cares of the world. Our Redeemer has said, "Peace I leave with you, my peace I give unto you: not as the world giveth, give I unto you. Let not your heart be troubled, neither let it be afraid" (John 14:27).

I will always remember the first time this very discernible peace came over me. I had just returned from Italy, traveling a memorable ten days with Scott. Upon returning home, I was faced with a stack of unread mail that needed attention. One of the first letters I opened was an invitation to attend the wedding reception for the son of one of my favorite cousins. Knowing that the mail had been sitting there for some time, I immediately became concerned that I might have missed the event. Quickly scanning the invitation, I was relieved to find that the reception was scheduled for Thursday evening. Evidently, I had one more day left.

Bright and early Thursday morning, Carolyn decided to begin her in-depth spring housecleaning. She was meticulous about our house, decorating and redecorating for every season and occasion. Her day was packed tightly with nonstop chores. In her mind, the last thing she wanted to do was stop her work, get cleaned up, and go to a wedding reception. To make matters worse, she decided at the last moment to personalize the wrapping of our gift to the newlyweds. This task took her more time than she had anticipated. The "time pressure" increased, and we could both feel it. And then it happened.

As she was struggling to wrap the gift, I became an observer. One moment I was there, totally involved in the frustration and stress, and the next I was literally just watching it as an observer, not as a participant. Fortunately for me, that same patient calmness followed me most of the evening. As time marched on, it became evident that I would need it.

The next dilemma came when, as the driver, I became lost on the way to the reception. I turned off on a newly completed freeway exit only to find we were miles away from our destination. My wife was not outwardly incriminating, but I sensed that inwardly she wished she were driving. Still holding on to that inner calm, I was neither frustrated nor critical of my mistake—nor did I blame the road crew for having opened a new exit. As a matter of fact, I found the whole experience rather interesting. I was fully enjoying the peace of eternal perspective in a situation that otherwise would have been frustrating.

When we finally arrived at the large, ten-story reception center, I dropped my wife off before entering the underground parking lot so she could find out where our particular reception was being held. My next challenge was simple—or so I thought. All I had to do was find a place to park the car. As I initiated my search, I found myself following an old out-of-state car that seemed twice the size of any available parking stalls. The elderly man behind the wheel was slowly and cautiously searching for a place that would accommodate his oversized carriage. As the amicable observer, I was gently amused. Where in the world would he put that enormous relic? How could I help? With a sense of unworldly calm, my own need to park took a backseat to the kind and patient concern I felt for the out-of-towner. I must confess that was not entirely like me.

Finally, miracle of miracles, he found a spot next to an entryway that allowed his oversized chariot to spill over the yellow parking lines. He began to maneuver his car by backing up and going forward over and over, each time positioning it for a more favorable attack until victory was his. I was delighted that he had won the battle. If it were not for the other cars backed up behind me, I might have stopped to congratulate him on his conquest. With a smile on my face, I was purposely replaying his victory over and over in my mind while I found my own place to park.

Meanwhile, my wife had entered a new level of personal frustration. There were many wedding receptions underway in the ten-story building that night, and she could not find the one to which we were invited. Were we at the wrong place? Did we have the wrong address or perhaps the wrong evening? Greatly annoyed, she telephoned a cousin to find out. Imagine how my wife must have felt about her husband when she learned that the reception was indeed on Thursday night—but two weeks hence.

At that moment, she was emotionally exhausted. She was also hungry, not having eaten since breakfast, something she often did when consumed with her tasks. She was also physically tired and outwardly frustrated at her husband's bungling efforts. All in all, she was not what my children would call "a happy camper." As for me, I was fine with the world. And why would I not be? I was still in the world but not of it.

While I was partly an observer, not caught up in the troubles of that night, I was also a peaceable participant. As we got on the elevator, instead of pressing the button that would take us to the parking garage, I selected the top floor that would take us to the well-known Roof Garden Restaurant atop the former grand hotel. There we enjoyed dinner together as the frustrating evening turned into an enjoyable date night.

After reading this tale, some of you may think, "Oh, all I have to do when I become frustrated and stressed is detach myself from the situation and become the 'observer.'" But feeling "detached" from others or yourself, either physically or emotionally, is not the same as feeling a divine peace that will grant you a safe and untroubled sense of "rightness," allowing your perception of trials to shift in a positive way.

Don't miss the point of the story. I believe that becoming the silent observer is the blessing of understanding our spiritual reality. We are not upset at the trivial, because we have a better understanding of the eternal scope of things. To prepare our inner selves for this peace, we peel away the outer layers of the natural man (our propensity to do evil) and view the world from a position of love. We are able to strip away those tribulations because we are so focused on being kind to others (and self) that there is not room for the natural man. We are able to receive that blessing because we have obeyed the law upon which that particular blessing is predicated (see D&C 130:20).

To be at God's peace is not a surreal state, as some might suggest. To the contrary, it creates clear discernment—an alert awareness of all that is going on and why it is going on. It does not depend on anything external to you except the recognition of your connection to divinity. It is not a fleeting experience but comes as an enduring sense of personal worth, along with a sense of rightness and safety. It is a state of freedom from grief and fear, from wanting and judging, from emotional negativity and toxicity. As we seek to be kind to others, God's kindness is bestowed upon us. It is in seeking after this unworldly peace that we find an overriding peace and spiritual happiness.

When we earnestly apply ourselves to think and do that which is good and uplifting, we pass rapidly through the slings and arrows that bring others down, arriving at a place where we can perceive what is true and virtuous with enlightened understanding. On this topic, Elder M. Russell Ballard quoted Benjamin Franklin, who said:

> Since the foundation of all happiness is thinking rightly, and since correct action is dependent on correct opinion, we cannot be too careful in choosing the value system we allow to govern our thoughts and actions.
>
> And to know that God governs in the affairs of men, that He hears and answers prayers, and that He is a rewarder of them that diligently seek Him, is indeed, a powerful regulator of human conduct.[56]

If your desires would have you continually reach out to that which is base and unworthy, you will fall to that very level and will not reach the

---

56   Quoted in Elder M. Russell Ballard, "Becoming Self-Reliant: Spiritually and Physically," *Ensign*, March 2009, 54.

tranquility spoken of here. In that ill-conceived condition, there can be no separation from the troubles of the world, in spite of your most earnest desires, for you have embraced that fatal attraction to the natural man. To rise above your base thoughts and desires, you must first cease to think and then do the things that brought you to that sad condition. Only then will the renewed circumstances that grow out of refined thought allow you to practice self-control over your thoughts and your actions. As Brigham Young taught, "The sooner an individual resists temptation to do, say, or think wrong, while he has light to correct his judgment, the quicker he will gain strength and power to overcome every temptation to evil."[57]

If we examine ourselves humbly and prayerfully, we can easily see that we do not always attract that which we want but that which we are. Who we are determines our thoughts, which in turn stimulates our desires—our desires feed on the "food" of our thoughts and actions, be they unclean or clean. Thus, to change who we are requires that we consciously change what we think.

This is often a challenge because it seems we are always more anxious to improve our circumstances (power, social standing, wealth) than we are to improve ourselves. By striving to change our worldly circumstances, we unwisely focus on those outward improvements. But of course, self-improvement is not outward. If you are to change your circumstances, first change yourself. By changing yourself, you may find that you have automatically changed your circumstances by viewing them differently, now understanding that you don't always need what you thought you needed to be happy. With the Lord's merciful support, you can find happiness now, despite life's trials.

Clearly, all refinement, all progress, and all love begin in the mind. Every seed sown and nurtured will one day take root and produce its own. Your task (and mine) is to make certain that the seeds sown are those that will bring forth good fruit. Clean thoughts produce clean actions. Unclean thoughts produce unclean actions. Control the mind and you will control your destiny.

---

57 *Journal of Discourses,* 6:94–95.

Chapter Fifteen
Understanding What Matters Most

One does not have to travel far to discover what matters most. The things that matter are all around us. I often saw them in the lives of those valiant souls who daily had to fight great adversity to overcome their grief. I admired them greatly. And out of their trials and tribulations came a better understanding of the things that matter most. After their victory, they had a different vision of life.

I recently read a book entitled *Silent Power* by Stuart Wilde. In it he explains that his martial arts teacher once told him that "when people go through the motion of walking, what they're doing, in effect, is going through a controlled fall. They lean forward with their upper bodies and throw out a leg just in time. That's why even a small crack in the pavement can tip them over."[58]

The last time I really stumbled on a proverbial crack in the pavement of my life, I was leaning forward with gusto—and I fell flat on my face. Without consulting anyone, I was busy planning all of the things that I wanted to do, trying to cleverly change the things I didn't like, and in general, I suspect, being a bit of a bore. I was so busy "doing" that I had forgotten that the main purpose in life was "being." Then, all of a sudden, a dull pain in my chest tripped me up, a "crack" that exposed my doing as an action not quite as important as I'd imagined. In a heartbeat (or lack thereof), all those things didn't matter so much anymore. This all took place in a flash when I suddenly realized I was having a heart attack.

As I was being rushed to the hospital, I realized that life is not just a time for doing, as important as that may be—particularly if one is doing righteous acts—but in the end, it is the *being* that counts most of all. If the

---

58 *Silent Power* (Carlsbad, CA: Hay House, 2005), 13.

being is in place, the *doing* will happen automatically. That understanding is part of the bigger picture I didn't see before.[59]

Thankfully, one does not have to have a heart attack to receive inspired awareness. For example, when I was in high school, I learned to play the saxophone and clarinet. A few years later, I even learned to play the string bass. After I was married, that acquired talent eventually led me to a part-time job playing in a small combo in the San Francisco Bay area. I really enjoyed playing with that group because they were great musicians.

One evening, after playing for an early wedding reception, we decided to go hear a well-known jazz group that was appearing in a nearby club. We entered the establishment and were soon seated at a table just a few feet away from the band. When they took a break, a couple of them sat down nearby and started up a conversation with us. Of course, the leader of our group had to tell them about out little combo. That did it. As they were to begin their next set, they announced over the microphone that some other musicians were in the audience. The audience started clapping, and the next thing I knew I was being pulled onto the bandstand to jam with them. Nervously, I propped up the man's bass and started to tentatively play with the group.

I was doing fairly well when the trumpet player took off on a wild riff. I followed him as best I could—then it happened. Out of nowhere, I entered a zone that I can best describe as "inspired awareness." Absolutely no conscious thoughts were connected to it, just an awareness of what each of the members of the group was doing and what each was going to do next. In that moment, I could "hear" the mellow notes coming from the tenor sax player before he even played them. I knew when the trumpet player was going to take over to do his own improvisation and where he was going with it. We were all in a synchronized zone because the music took us there. I no longer thought about the audience, my playing, or anything else. In fact, I had no overt thoughts at all. I was in a new inspired zone of awareness along with the rest of the band and played accordingly. When it was over, I came out of my "unconsciousness" to the wild clapping of the audience. When I returned to our table, my friends asked me, "Wow! Where did that come from?" I softly replied, "I have no idea." This is not to be confused with what we talked about in chapter five, where simply allowing our thoughts to choose the direction of our lives without understanding where that choice will lead can be life threatening.

59　See Lynn G. Robbins, "What Manner of Men and Women Ought Ye to Be?" *Ensign*, April 2011.

Instead, this experience could be described as being hyperfocused almost in a different dimension, the dimension of the spirit.

When I "met" those other musicians in our shared state of awareness, an immediate and deep relationship was formed. So much so that when I left the club that evening, the strangers in the band, people whose names I didn't even know, hugged me tightly—and I hugged them as if we had been good friends for years. We had to. We had grown too close to merely walk away from each other with just a wave or a handshake. We had formed a bond I will always remember.

I tell you my jazz story not to brag about my forgotten musical talents (as much as my ego might enjoy that) but as a preamble to what really happened that night. It is hard to describe, but it is similar to the stories I have read about people who have had near-death experiences. I did not die, nor did I have an out-of-body experience. What did take place, however, was a profound, quick immersion into pure musical inspiration. In those relatively few minutes, my musical talents were expanded far beyond my normal capacity. It was as if I had been previously endowed with advanced musical talent, temporarily hidden away and forgotten, but then spiritually brought forward in that one marvelous moment. I experienced in one improvised tune something of the bigger picture of my life—a part of my life that I didn't even know. The more I pondered that experience, the more I felt a spiritual understanding of the divinity that is in us all. The music I played that evening was only a vehicle to take me to this deeper understanding. I came to realize that words such as *spiritual enlightenment* and *illumination* (which I previously thought only of as words) are, in fact, actual concepts.

When I entered that spiritual zone of awareness, I not only went to a deeper level of understanding and knowledge but to a deeper and different level of happiness than I had ever before experienced. It was as if everything was love. That evening everyone in that musical group loved me, and I loved them in spite of the fact that we had never met. That love not only enveloped us as individuals but seemed to permeate everything and everyone around me. That experience left me with a particular feeling of joy that I had never experienced before, and all I wanted to do was bask in its radiance. It stayed with me all the way home that evening. I could think of and feel nothing else.

I learned from that experience is that God is love. I don't mean that He isn't a divine personage. He is that, to be sure. But I also learned that He loves me and you more than I ever thought possible. And that evening, with

His love, I too was filled with love . . . for Him and for all others. In that brief period of time there were no unkind or negative thoughts or feelings possible. In my special moment with those other musicians, I recognized that our purpose is to learn to be like Him.

My ultracreative musical experience happened only once, but from that event (and other nonmusical events), I learned that a deeper level of pure spiritual understanding and love are available to us if we will but enter into that realm. I have since found that I can have similar experiences whenever I want—not as dramatic, nor at the same level, but they do provide for me that same understanding. For example, as I look out at the sunrise or anything else in God's creation, I don't have to say, "Isn't that beautiful?" (I have learned that words often interfere with spiritual understanding.) I just recognize that I am a part of the great creation I see before me. Viewing that magnificent vista, I am reminded that just as God the Father and God the Son are one in Their glorious purpose, I too am part of that purpose—to help "bring to pass the immortality and eternal life of man" (Moses 1:39). With that understanding, viewing God's creations brings a profound sense of being connected to divinity with my own heavenly purpose.

I also learned that mind-dominated relationships lack the deeper connection that comes through inspired awareness, such as I had experienced that evening. The mind brings forth all kinds of expectations of those who are waiting for their love to be fulfilled. But true love is found in being aware of the needs of others, not because one partner has analyzed the needs of the other but because one simply "knows" what others need by divine inspiration, just as I knew in advance what the trumpet player needed me to do and he knew what I needed from him.

In a mind-dominated relationship, a husband might think, "All I want is to be loved and appreciated." Of course, he would then think of all the things that he would want his wife to do to prove to him that he was really loved and appreciated. Her failure to meet any of those expectations, however unrealistic, would undoubtedly cause some grief. As we discussed earlier, unmet expectations often do that. If all of his expectations were not met, he would probably feel obligated to mention to his wife that she was not meeting his needs, which could prove frustrating and hurtful to her. And thus it goes.

But spiritual awareness of the bigger picture of life bypasses such a supposed "need list" and goes directly to the heart. It is not conceived or thought of, because there is no need. True love takes care of everything through its spiritual awareness. It is in going beyond your thoughts that you become cognizant of the needs of others. You "see" them in your awareness and know more clearly why your partner thinks and behaves the way he or she does. By becoming "aware," you become compassionate, forgiving, patient, loving, and many other virtues come into play because the Spirit awakens this knowledge. Your own selfish need list disappears as it is replaced with the happiness of living in that state of awareness.

The kind of inspiration that came to me that night in a jazz club is not unique to me. I am certain you too have had moments of pure inspiration given to you for your own personal development or protection. For example, a man I know and greatly admire was a B-17 bomber pilot in World War II. He shared with a small group of us an experience he had while on military assignment.

It seems he and his crew left Tokyo, flying south over the Pacific, not knowing they were headed into a typhoon. They had been flying several hours when the navigator announced on the intercom that they had been blown off course (flying then was not like flying is today). My friend decided to drop down through the cloud cover with the hope of sighting land. However, the only thing he could see was ocean, white with churning waves. Then, to make matters worse, their long-range radio went out. Trying to find their bearings, they began flying an expanding grid-search so they would know they were covering new territory, not just flying in a circle. After some time, the copilot suggested that it was time to turn, but something inside my friend whispered for him to continue on. He responded, "Hold it steady for a few more minutes."

They were flying just a few thousand feet above the water when, suddenly, he saw a long line of white waves crashing over some rocks protruding out of the ocean. It meant they had to be close to an island. But they did not know if the island was on the north or south side of the rocks. He prayerfully made a turn and, after about five minutes, picked up voices on their portable short-range radio. Following the strength of that signal, they soon saw what turned out to be Tinian Island and were able to land. Just as they began taxiing down the runway, the plane's engines shut down one by one. They were totally out of gas.

My friend came back from that journey far out in the Pacific with a renewed witness that God exists and that He whispered inspiration to him, saving all of their lives. What he learned, and what we also need to learn, is to always stay His course—to do those things that will allow the Spirit to also whisper lifesaving instructions to us. Like my pilot friend, our eternal lives depend on it.

As previously mentioned, there are basically two kinds of knowledge—one that comes from the mind and the other that comes from the Spirit. While these two kinds of knowledge are separate and distinct, they are also companions. In the case of my pilot friend, his secular knowledge taught him how to fly the plane, but it was his spiritual understanding that told him where to go in order to save their lives. One reflects the here and now—the other the then and there. The one reflects the minutia of daily living—the other the "big picture," the purpose of life. Together they form a more perfect understanding.

While the one kind of knowledge without the other is not complete, it is the spiritual, with its luminous flashes of insight and comprehension, that makes the inspired goal visible. As the Savior emphasized, "Seek ye first the kingdom of God, and his righteousness; and all these things shall be added unto you" (Matt. 6:33). Seek first for spiritual understanding, and as you do so, the secular learning—acquired from the best of books and teachings—will automatically be sifted like fine flour into the "baker's mix," producing a superior-tasting loaf when baked in the oven of faith and works.

This newly acquired inspiration makes clear that "the natural man receiveth not the things of the Spirit of God: for they are foolishness unto him: neither can he know them, because they are spiritually discerned" (1 Cor. 2:14).

It is through this step-by-step process that spiritual understanding will replace the "unanswerable." By living one truth, others will appear, thus expanding our ability to receive further light and knowledge, because all truths are interconnected and interdependent. As we receive spiritual understanding, making our perspective clear, we should seek for the Spirit's governing principle related to our needs—for one governing principle is always linked to a wide variety of other governing principles. To understand one is to understand the many that appear in a never-ending linkage, leading us along the narrow path to what matters most—the thoughts, actions, and relationships that will bring us lasting happiness.

Spiritual understanding, with its accompanying peace, often does not come all at once but rather arrives "line upon line," thus allowing us to develop and mature, little by little, into an ever-growing understanding and happiness. After all, it is after the trial that the miracle appears; it is after the struggle that we see things more clearly. As the prophet Moroni wrote, "I would show unto the world that faith is things which are hoped for and not seen; wherefore, dispute not because ye see not, for ye receive no witness until after the trial of your faith" (Ether 12:6).

Without the struggle, we would have no point of reference upon which to value the knowledge received. It is in experiencing the struggle that we come to appreciate its gift. As Brigham Young once taught:

> If the Saints could realize things as they are when they are called to pass through trials, and to suffer what they call sacrifices, they would acknowledge them to be the greatest blessings that could be bestowed upon them. But put them in possession of true principles and true enjoyments, without the opposite, and they could not know enjoyment, they could not realize happiness. They could not tell light from darkness, because they have no knowledge of darkness and consequently are destitute of a realizing sense of light. If they should not taste the bitter, how could they realize the sweet? They could not.[60]

One important concept to remember when searching for that which matters most is that if a thought doesn't edify, it is dangerous to pursue. By harkening to that counsel you will become more and more tuned toward His will, becoming the recipient of the love and light of Christ each day.

When the early elders of the restored Church became confused by the "false spirits" that "have gone forth in the earth" (D&C 50:1), the Lord advised promptly, "When a man reasoneth he is understood of man, because he reasoneth as a man; even so will I, the Lord, reason with you that you may understand" because "that which doth not edify is not of God, and is darkness" (D&C 50:12, 23). This time-proven principle is simple: if you always choose to think and then to do that which edifies, your level of confidence in making correct decisions is greatly enhanced. Likewise, if you choose to think and then to do that which does not edify, your level of confidence in making good judgments is greatly weakened. Remember, to overcome the serendipity and the foolishness of an impulsive mind, "seek ye first the kingdom of God" (3 Ne. 13:33). This is one of those time-tested governing laws that will guide you through innumerable choices.

---

60 *Journal of Discourses*, 2:302.

Hard decisions require careful and insightful consideration. Therefore, we should be aware that being light-minded—not being mindful of "the Light"—detracts from our attempt to garnish our thoughts with righteousness as we seek for a higher spiritual consciousness of what is right and what is wrong. To be able to see where we are going, we must stay in the Light of Christ and shun the dark shadows cast by the natural man.

Wisdom, the ability to identify what matters most, is not necessarily age related. Recall Christ's admonition that unless we become as little children, we cannot enter the kingdom of heaven. It is in the innocence of a child that wisdom can more easily take root—something often impossible in the dark, contaminated mind of the wayward or simply preoccupied adult. But young or old, it is through the Spirit, accessible only through "pure hearts and clean hands" (2 Ne. 25:16) that the mysteries of life are made manifest. It is in understanding and obeying the "law upon which all blessings are predicated" that "we obtain any blessing from God" (D&C 130:20, 21)—making us wise as well as blessed.

At times in our lives, we may feel lost and afraid. But that does not mean we are lost to Him. We may be exactly where we need to be. Remember that it was Christ who questioned, "My God, why has thou forsaken me?" (Matt. 27:46) when He was doing precisely what God wanted Him to be doing: atoning for our sins. We are in this life, with all of its challenges, because that is exactly where we need to be—where we can best learn truth. We cannot grow without the spiritual understanding of truth because "it is impossible for a man to be saved in ignorance" (D&C 131:6). Ignorance, even in innocence, cannot sustain us any more than Adam's innocence sustained his growth and development.

Chapter Sixteen

CONCLUSION

GUIDING PRINCIPLES

APPROPRIATELY, THE TITLE OF THIS final chapter is "Conclusion." The word means to bring together a logical summation of the facts that have been presented. It also implies that an ending condition has been reached. Hence, the purpose of this final chapter is to bring together a summation of facts that may well hold the key to the ending of the condition of one's self-imposed grief as well as the beginning of increased spiritual understanding and happiness.

As a reference, remember that my own grief came to a conclusion only when I had the facts—when I understood that because of my misplaced anger at Carolyn's doctor, I had allowed my toxic thoughts to multiply, locking me into a state of grief from which I could see no conclusion (things seem to go on and on if they are not understood). Succinctly stated, the truth cannot set you free unless you know what the truth is. Finally, when I specifically understood what was causing my grief, I simply quit doing those things, thus enabling me to "conclude" (put an end to) my grief and start a new life.

Thus we see that conclusions have two aspects: the end of something and the beginning of something else. It is for us to decide if our conclusions in this work mark the end of good things and the beginning of bad things or if they mark the end of bad things and the beginning of good things.

For example, the Book of Mormon is replete with both good and bad conclusions—of contention and wars and peace and prosperity. Those who gained testimonies of God concluded their warring ways and were happy; those who did not believe in Him provoked wars and were unhappy.

Knowing the facts and living accordingly can be a valid, life-changing concept for the individual who wants to escape his grief, as well as for the many "who have dwindled in unbelief" (Morm. 9:35). This concept is reflected in all things because opposition in all things is only mitigated with the truth—the facts. Hence, the concepts contained herein are not just for the individual but also for the masses.

OVERCOMING YOUR GRIEF

As we consider the relevant facts presented in this book—facts that can assist you in attaining your release from grief—we may conclude that:

1. Negative thoughts can often create grief. Hence, we would do well to be selective in our thoughts in order to control our grief. As we do so, we can accept the facts of our reality and move on. Those who do not accept "what is" are too often destined to remain in a self-imposed state of grief (see chapters 1 and 2).

2. The realization of any desired end is based on the selection of thoughts that can make it happen, for a runaway mind often confuses the ends with the means and fosters false perceptions, illusions, and fantasies of fear. To the contrary, when the mind is focused, it produces. If we allow our negative thoughts to control our lives, we can become our misguided thoughts. This condition weakens our resolve and diminishes our agency. It should be vigorously guarded against (see chapter 2).

3. Our grief is often triggered by one or more toxic thoughts that create an avalanche of additional false perceptions and negative thoughts. Find your negative trigger points and eliminate them from your life. In like manner, you should also find your positive trigger points and showcase them. The more we focus on the positive trigger points, the less the negative points appear.

If what we experience does not result in what we want, we may attempt to emphasize certain parts and deemphasize or ignore others, thus distorting our thoughts. These distorted thoughts often create a powerful illusion of truth because they "feel" right (what we think is what we believe). However, since the mind feeds on feelings, the distance between what you feel and what is truth can be ever increasing, particularly when your feelings are shrouded in grief.

One solution to this dilemma is if your perception makes you unhappy, despondent, blue, dejected, downhearted, pessimistic, or any similar feeling that brings you down, challenge it. Find the truth! Do not overgeneralize events or deemphasize or disqualify things (see chapter 3).

4. Our thoughts often erroneously define who we are: "I am a farmer," "I am a musician," "I am a housewife," "I am a teacher." Of course, we may

do what is required to fulfill these vocations, but we are *not* our jobs. Others may negatively define themselves as fat or skinny, tall or short, but that isn't who they are either. They are not their bodies. Then there are those who negatively define themselves as worthless or any number of other self-destructive definitions. But those definitions are also not who they are. Simply recognize that these negative thoughts are ill-conceived invasions feeding off the negativity they generate. Eliminate these erroneous definitions from your life (see chapter 4).

5. If we are to enjoy our lives, we must be "present," not lost in the negative thoughts and actions of the past. If we spend our time thinking of a toxic past or of a future filled with fear, we can miss a goodly and enjoyable part of our lives. Live in the now and enjoy what is. Put an expiration date on all of the bad memories that serve no purpose and get rid of them (see chapter 5).

6. Negative judgment of others brings with it a resulting counter judgment. Both the judgment and the counter judgment can produce grief. If we would rid ourselves of this danger, we would do well to shun judging others, for when we judge others, we provoke our own swift judgment, not only for our actions but for our thoughts as well.

Tucked neatly into the folds of judgment and its related grief is the absolute need to forgive others. Without forgiveness, the judgment often goes on and on—as does the mind with its negative thoughts, creating a major source of grief. But if you forgive others, any accompanying grief that was once associated with that past event is done away with. It disappears (see chapter 6).

7. When we conjure up expectations that are unmet, we often become dissatisfied and unhappy. Sometimes we feel discouraged in not having our expectations met because of the greed, meanness, or deceit of someone else. We bow under the heaviness of our misfortunes that others have created for us. "It is wrong," we say. "It's not fair." "It is cruel and unjust." "Why did this happen to me?" And in the agony and intensity of our feelings, we almost unconsciously repeat the words over and over again in monotonous reiteration, as if in some way that repetition might bring relief.

To protect us from such we should make certain that our expectations are based upon those things of divine importance and not the things that our pride "says" we need. That simple distinction will often keep unmet expectations at bay (see chapter 7).

8. Self-deception continually causes grief for those who practice it. The individual who knowingly blames others for something he did will surely

double his error and grief. In trying to deceive others, he also deceives himself.

The natural man in us works through the mind to justify the spiraling descent we see in today's world as always existing "out there" instead of *within* each of us. If everyone believes it to be "out there" (it's the "natural" thing to do), there can be neither accountability nor identification of the true source of one's problems. The sin, the mistake, the error, or whatever it is that keeps us from reaching our highest potential rarely originates "out there." It originates from within. Those who take responsibility and pray to accept what cannot be changed can eliminate self-deception from their lives (see chapter 8).

9. The worry and fear of what *might* be (things that rarely come to pass) can create an inordinate amount of unnecessary grief in our lives. There is no limit to what grief our fearful thoughts may generate. Such thoughts tell us we may lose our jobs, our sweetheart, our health, our everything. These thoughts can cause paranoia, stress, obsession, jealousy, and neurotic disorders. It limits the faith of our vision, growth, and personal development. Our fear of not being good enough, big enough, thin enough, humble enough, proud enough, smart enough, or rich enough creates nothing but trouble. Some of our fearful thoughts are real, but when carefully examined, we will find that most thoughts are imaginary and lead us only to grief (see chapter 9).

INCREASING YOUR HAPPINESS

10. The spiritual knowledge we once had but is now forgotten is in the repository of our spiritual understanding. We may not remember, but we can still feel at least a sliver of truth without understanding why or even how we know something to be true. Spiritual understanding is a gift given as an answer to prayer or as a divine response to a specific need that may or may not be requested or even known. It comes by way of inspired confirmations as truth is miraculously revealed.

If we learn to walk in His ways, we will learn to understand His thoughts, His reasoning, and His logic, and our happiness is increased. It is then that the unanswerable questions of the world become revealed as reasonable and logical because they will have been explained by the Spirit (see chapter 10).

11. It is self-evident that our pain is not felt in the past or in the future but in the present. It is also self-evident that happiness can only be enjoyed in the now. In comparison, the negative power of the mind, that which

provokes grief, lives mainly in the past because that is where it gets its "food" for its negative and painful thoughts. If you have to call on the past or the future, don't make your stay long. Do what you need to do and then get back to the present. To increase your happiness, live in the now (see chapter 11).

12. As you overcome your grief, you will change your world for the better. We understand from the Lord's greatest commandment that the key for that is love. But how to truly love remains somewhat vague and is certainly subject to interpretation. A more straightforward and simple formula is to be kind to everything and everyone, including oneself, all the time, with no exceptions. Being kind to every*thing* takes on new meaning when we understand that all things were first created spiritually. This time-proven method then provides a road map to spiritual growth and happiness (see chapter 12).

13. Kindness is the connecting link to a multitude of virtues. If you were to focus each day on being kind, you would soon witness how those connections are made. This state of spiritual connectedness provides clarity of who we are as well as our relationship and responsibilities to others. It creates peace, joy, and happiness. It is in this manner that you can change your world—and the world of others (see chapter 13).

14. As you consistently apply the principles contained herein, you will find increased clarity of mind. Rising above the clamor of the world, you will feel at peace, often becoming the patient observer, as it were, witnessing all that is going on without making unrighteous judgments or feeling fear. During those moments, you will become untroubled by the frustrating cares of the world. You will find peace—God's peace (see chapter 14).

15. Just as God the Father and God the Son are one in Their glorious purpose, we too are part of that purpose—to help "bring to pass the immortality and eternal life of man" (Moses 1:39). That knowledge allows us a glimpse of what matters most. Armed with this spiritual understanding we are able to put aside those things that matter little to focus on those things that have eternal consequence (see chapter 15).

As you read these fifteen governing principles, remember that clarification of any of these can be easily referenced in its corresponding chapter. In this manner, you can use the book both as a general handbook as well as a reference guide to be consulted as often as is desired.

As a concluding suggestion, I ask you to consider one of the fifteen guidelines and focus on that principle for a chosen period of time. For example, you might begin by saying, "Today I will make certain to accept that which I cannot change." Then tomorrow, you might resolve, "Today I will not allow my thoughts to govern me, but I will govern my thoughts." Daily do one of these exercises for each of the fifteen governing principles. When you finish, simply start over. As you continue to employ these exercises, you will find that you are automatically living all of the guiding principles provided in this book. As they become second nature to you, they will also become those laudable characteristics mentioned herein. Then you will assuredly know that they work as you find yourself living with increased joy, happiness, and peace to your soul (the other side of grief) as any self-imposed grief melts away like the morning dew.

I have made mention several times in this book that all truths are circumscribed into one great whole. Hence, all truths are interdependent and, of course, interrelated. Therefore, as you find one truth, others in that relationship will also be revealed. The fifteen mentioned here are only the tip of the iceberg. Go forth and find other principles that are more unique to you and yours and trumpet them forth from the housetops.

Good luck, and God bless you.

About the Author

 Dr. Joseph Layton Bishop Jr. was born in the small farming community of Delta, Utah. Among the many things he learned while on the farm was that farmers could not then and cannot now control the early and late frosts, the untimely raging rains, or the fierce winds that often blow newly mown hay into the next county. One cold wintry night, while struggling to dam up an overflowing irrigation ditch (with ice-cold water pouring into his mud-entombed boot all the while), he made a life-changing decision: he was not going to be a farmer. He was going to be a university professor. The next year he unceremoniously left the farm to pursue his goal.

Later, his career path quickly led him from teaching into administrative positions. He cut his first administrative teeth as the director of the Haitian-American Institute in Port-au-Prince, Haiti. He later accepted a position as director of instruction at Mt. San Jacinto College in Hemet, California. Following that, he accepted a position as academic vice president of the newly created Prairie State College in Chicago Heights, Illinois. Later he became the executive director of a consortium of progressive colleges called GT-70, based in Miami, Florida. Subsequently, he was offered the post of president of Weber State College in Ogden, Utah.

Near the end of his administration at Weber State, he received a call from the Church to be the president of the Buenos Aires North Mission in Argentina, the same country he had served in as a young man. After his mission, the Church again called him to serve, this time as president of the Missionary Training Center in Provo. After his three-year assignment there, he accepted a position as associate professor at Brigham Young University. That position allowed him time to do some meaningful research, the results of which are directly reflected in this book. He later served two additional missions for the Church, one as the area welfare agent for Central America and one as acting president of the Samoa Apia Mission.

He is married to Rena M. Davis, a retired nurse, and between the two of them, they have ten children, more grandchildren than they ever could have wished for, and a few great-grandchildren. Both now retired, they live in beautiful St. George, Utah.